EARLY
TUDOR COMPOSERS

Oxford Musical Essays

Early Tudor Composers

Biographical sketches of thirty-two musicians and
composers of the period 1485-1555

WITH A PREFACE BY

SIR W. HENRY HADOW, C.B.E., Mus.D.
Vice-Chancellor of Sheffield University

By WILLIAM H. GRATTAN FLOOD

Hon. Mus.D., National University of Ireland

Essay Index Reprint Series

Originally published by:
OXFORD UNIVERSITY PRESS

BOOKS FOR LIBRARIES PRESS
FREEPORT, NEW YORK

First Published 1925
Reprinted 1968

927.8
A33e

Reprinted from a copy in the collections of
The Brooklyn Public Library

INTERNATIONAL STANDARD BOOK NUMBER:
0-8369-0447-8

LIBRARY OF CONGRESS CATALOG CARD NUMBER:
68-25603

PRINTED IN THE UNITED STATES OF AMERICA

80-427

DEDICATED TO

MR. H. B. COLLINS, Mus. Bac., F.R.C.O.

IN RECOGNITION OF MUCH VALUED HELP IN

THE PREPARATION OF THIS VOLUME

NOTE

THIS series of articles, which is now recast and revised, appeared in the *Musical Times*, sporadically, between November 1919 and June 1924, and is published under one cover with the permission of Messrs. Novello & Co., Ltd. The biographies (thirty-two) are based on independent research, carried out under much difficulty, and of these at least twenty were hitherto a blank, proving quite elusive for our musical historians. With the revived interest in Tudor music the sketches of the lives of these men, especially of such giants as Aston, Redford, Ludford, Pasche, Fayrfax, Newark, Ashwell, and Davy, will, I feel sure, prove acceptable to those who would fain know something of the English school that developed naturally with the full-tide glory of the golden age of Taverner, Tallis, Byrd, Tyre, White, Gibbons, and others. In this connexion, the initiative of Sir Henry Hadow, in the magnificent quarto volumes of *Tudor Church Music* edited by a devoted quartet of enthusiasts with meticulous care and published for the Trustees of the Carnegie United Kingdom Trust by the Oxford University Press, must compel the admiration and gratitude of all lovers of Tudor music.

W. H. GRATTAN FLOOD

September 1924

PREFACE

No event in musical history is more important than the discovery of our lost Tudor compositions. There have been other salient instances of loss and neglect—Bach's B Minor Mass was first performed ninety-five years after it was written ; Schubert's posthumous works outnumber by ten to one those published in his lifetime—but there has been no other case in which a people with a great musical position has allowed it to lapse entirely for three centuries, and during this time has contentedly borne the reproach of unproductiveness. A generation ago the available amount of Tudor music was confined to a few slender volumes ill-edited and misunderstood : now the number of compositions published or ready for publication probably exceeds a thousand.

The causes of the loss are not difficult to determine. None of the Tudor music was printed in score ; part books were easily mutilated or mislaid, the fashion of music underwent in the seventeenth century a series of rapid changes, the old polyphony became obsolete, by the beginning of the nineteenth century the speech of Byrd and Tallis was treated almost as a dead language. The well-meant but misdirected efforts of the Musical Antiquarian Society only rendered obscure what was already unfamiliar : the Church music shrank to a few anthems, the madrigals were forced into metrical systems for which they had never been intended, the clavier pieces were laid aside, with the harpsichord, in the dusty corners of the museum. It is not too much to say that any one who, thirty years ago, had estimated our Tudor

8

Preface

composers at their true value, would have been received with incredulity and in all probability with ridicule.

The discovery of the lost treasure was effected by a band of devoted scholars and artists—Squire, Fuller-Maitland, Arkwright, Collins, and the committee of experts who, with wider opportunity and ampler resources, are now employed upon the great Carnegie edition. Of their labours such monuments have already appeared as the Fitzwilliam Virginal book, Dr. Fellowes's definitive edition of the madrigals, now complete, the Masses of William Byrd and of some of his contemporaries or predecessors, an increasing amount of miscellaneous Church music, and the first three Carnegie volumes, two of which are devoted to Taverner and the third to a selection of William Byrd's English Church compositions. When the task is complete we shall realize, perhaps with some lingering surprise, that here is an achievement which may without exaggeration be set in comparison with that of the Elizabethan drama.

Among the scholars who have materially helped to elucidate this period, an honourable place has been won by Dr. Grattan Flood. He has occupied many years in researches, often difficult and remote, with a view to rescuing from undeserved oblivion many artists who advanced the cause of English music at the time of its highest renown. It is probably beyond the reach of hope that we should recover all the names—some of the most beautiful compositions are anonymous and the internal evidence is not always strong enough for certain attribution—for the list given in this volume we are highly indebted to Dr. Grattan Flood's wide knowledge and untiring industry. In some cases he has succeeded in correcting errors that had become almost inveterate, as in the restoration to one William Cornish of the works which

Preface

previous historians had conjecturally distributed between two. Elsewhere he has considerably added to our knowledge of composers whose names were already in some currency, as for instance Fayrfax, Ludford, Davy, and Thomas Farthing. But most of all he has earned our gratitude by supplying biographical details of men about whom practically nothing was known : men whose names were as fleeting and unsubstantial as the ghosts in the *Odyssey*, and to whom he has given the reviving draught that has restored them to some semblance of warmth and life. On all grounds alike his volume is a valuable contribution to musical biography ; it will be indispensable to the musical historian of the future.

W. H. HADOW.

CONTENTS

Contents

I. Gilbert Banaster

It is strange that the history of the English Chapel Royal has not yet been adequately treated, save for the account given in Rimbault's *Cheque Book of the Chapel Royal* (1870), which, however, begins only with the year 1485. Yet Gilbert Banaster deserves to be held in remembrance as a distinguished Master of the Choristers of the Chapel Royal, as well as an early Tudor composer. His predecessor, Henry Abyngdon, had been Master from 1455 to 1478, and had made the singers of the Chapel Royal famous, so much so, that in October 1471, Galeazzo Maria Sforza, Duke of Milan, had sent his Chapel Master (Rayner) to pick out some good English singers and musicians for Milan (*Calendar of State Papers*, Milan, p. 161).

Up to the present the only account of Banaster is the brief notice of G. E. P. Arkwright, in the second edition of Grove's *Dictionary of Music and Musicians* (vol. i, p. 179). Henry Davey, in his *History of English Music* (new edition, 1921), dismisses Banaster in a couple of lines, although acknowledging that he was an 'important composer of the later 15th century'; and he insinuates that his Mastership of the Children of the Chapel Royal began only in 1482, this being, in reality, the date of the confirmation of his appointment.

Gilbert Banaster (whose name also appears as Banester and Banastre) was born *circa* 1445, and on September 29, 1478, was appointed Master of the Children of the Chapel Royal. He is said to have been a son of Henry Banaster, Yeoman of the Crown, who died in 1456, and it is not unlikely that he was a boy of the Chapel Royal, under Henry Abyngdon, becoming a Gentleman of the Chapel in 1475, the same time as William Newark.

Banaster's appointment as Master was formally ratified by Patent under Privy Seal dated Westminster, February 6, 1478/9, and is thus summarized in the printed *Calendar of Patent Rolls* of Edward IV (p. 133) :

> Grant to Gilbert Banaster of forty marks yearly from the petty custom in the port of London and ports and places adjacent for the maintenance, instruction, and governance of the boys of the Chapel of the Household from Michaelmas last, on which day he undertook these, so long as he shall have the same.

This grant was confirmed by the Act of Resumption, on February 28, 1482/3.

Edward IV held Banaster in high esteem, and in 1481 granted him a corrody in the Priory of Holy Trinity, Norwich, confirmed to him on May 10, 1482 (*Cal. Pat. Rolls, Edward IV*, p. 307). He subsequently held corrodies from the Abbey of St. Benet Hulme and the Abbey of Bardney.

Richard III also appreciated Banaster, and in the second year of his reign, September 16, 1484, issued a commission to John Melynek, Gentleman of the Chapel Royal, to impress men and boys for the King's Chapel. Under this commission, Melynek was empowered

> . . . to take and seize for the King all such singing men and children expert in the science of music, within all places of the realm, as well in cathedral churches, colleges, chapels, houses of religion, and all other franchised or exempt places, or elsewhere.

This grant has been incorrectly quoted by previous writers, and Rimbault gives the date 1485 instead of 1484. The original manuscript of the grant will be found in the British Museum among the Harleian MSS. (433, fol. 189).

Richard III died on August 22, 1485 (Battle of Bosworth), and Henry VII effected the union of the two roses of York and Lancaster by his marriage, on January 17, 1486, to Elizabeth of York. By the Act of Resumption, Banaster had been confirmed in his patent ' for the exhibition, instruction, and governance of

Gilbert Banaster

the children of the Chapel '. The number of children at this date was ten, and continued to be so all through this king's reign.

As was to be expected, the marriage of Henry VII was the occasion of great celebrations. A long Latin Epithalamium was written by John de Gigliis, afterwards Bishop of Worcester, and a Latin Anthem in five parts, ' O Maria et Elizabeth ', was composed by Banaster. This fine composition is now in the Eton College Library, and deserves the attention of the Carnegie Trust. It is interesting to add that there was also written an English anthem, set to music by Thomas Ashwell [1] on this memorable occasion, commencing :

> God save King Herry wheresoe'er he be,
> And for Queen Elizabeth now pray we,
> And for all her noble progeny.
> God save the Church of Christ from any folly,
> And for Queen Elizabeth now pray we.

After the marriage ceremony the King showed his appreciation of the services of the Chapel Royal by conferring various grants and corrodies on some of the Gentlemen, including William Newark and Thomas Worley. A new Dean was appointed in the person of Richard Hill, who on the Feast of Corpus Christi, 1486, permitted ' the singers of the King's Chapel ' to assist at evening devotions in the Church of St. Margaret's, Westminster, under their Master, Gilbert Banaster. The King also made a grant to the Sub-Dean of the Chapel, Richard Surland, of the free chapel of St. Peter in the Tower of London.

In the autumn of the year 1486 Banaster fell ill, and his post as Master was temporarily filled by Laurence Squire, a priest-musician. Not long afterwards he retired formally, and a patent, during pleasure, was granted to Squire, at an annual salary of forty marks, on November 8, 1486. Banaster made his will on August 19, 1487, and died a few days later. His will was proved on January 31, 1488, and his three corrodies were granted

[1] See later, p. 55 *seq.*

15

(September 1, 1487) to Edward Jones, William Newark, and Thomas Worley respectively.

Banaster was not only a composer but a poet, and there is still preserved a manuscript ' Miracle of St. Thomas ' in Benet College Library, dated 1467, consisting of five seven-lined stanzas. The manuscript forms part of the Chronicle of John Stone, ' Monk of Christ Church, Canterbury, 1467 '.

Among the compositions of Banaster still preserved are two charming motets in the Pepys Collection, 1236, in the Magdalene College Library, Cambridge. One of these is a three-part ' Vos secli justi judices ', the other a two-part ' Alleluia, Laudate '. The Fayrfax MS., now in the British Museum (Add. MSS. 5468), contains one secular song by Banaster, namely, ' My feerful dreme '.

Mr. G. E. P. Arkwright says that Banaster ' belongs to the school which is seen at its best in the work of Dr. Fayrfax ', and this opinion from an expert in Tudor music should be an incentive to the publication of the magnificent Fayrfax MS., which contains forty-nine songs to secular words for three or four voices.

II. *David Burton*

AMONG the many eminent English composers of the early Tudor period David Burton occupies a high place, and yet up to the present his biography has presented little more than conjecture. In the dozen lines accorded to him in the new edition of Grove's *Dictionary of Music* (vol. i, p. 425) his name appears as 'Avery Burton'. A brief notice is also given him under the name of Avery (vol. i, p. 138) by Mr. J. F. N. Stainer. Mr. G. E. P. Arkwright says that he may be identified with the Awrie whom Morley names in his list of authorities (*Plaine and Easie Intro-duction*, 1597), whose name, 'Master Avere', appears as composer of a 'Te Deum' for the organ in Brit. Mus. Add. MS. 29976. It also adds that a five-part Mass by him ('Ut Re Mi Fa Sol La') is in the Forest-Heyther Collection, Oxford Music School Collec-tion (MS. Mus. Sch. E. 376–381), and notes that 'the name of "Davy" Burton appears in the list of Henry VIII's Chapel, 1520'.

From a close search of the State Papers the following entries throw new light on the high estimation in which David Burton was no doubt held, testifying to his powers as a musician and composer.

Mr. Arkwright's surmise as to the identity of 'Davy' Burton with 'Aubree' or Avery Burton is amply substantiated by official records ; in fact his name appears in four varying forms, namely, David Burton, Davy Burton, Avery Burton, and Avery Burnett —also as 'Davy', 'Avery', and 'Burton'.

The first notice of this distinguished musician is in 1494, when we find him as the recipient of the then respectable *douceur* of twenty shillings for composing a Mass. This record appears in the Privy Purse expenses of Henry, in which the brief entry is chronicled as follows in 'To Burton, for making a Mass, 20*s*.' under date of November 29, 1494.

Early Tudor Composers

Fifteen years later, in November 1509, David Burton was appointed a Gentleman of the Chapel Royal, filling the vacancy created by the promotion of William Cornish as Master of the Children, in succession to William Newark, deceased. He received livery for the funeral of Prince Henry on February 22, 1511. Not long afterwards, on August 16, he received a lucrative emolument as Keeper of Chestren Wood, Kent, *vice* John Pende, deceased. This office was confirmed to him on April 1, 1512, when an order was made that he was to be paid ' 2*d*. a day and arrears from 16 August last '.

On June 20, 1513, Burton crossed the Channel with the rest of the Chapel Royal in the train of King Henry VIII, and we read that on September 17, after the High Mass was sung at Tournai, the ' Te Deum ' was performed by the English singers, followed by a sermon by Edmund Birkhead, bishop of St. Asaph. A fortnight previously the English Chapel Royal sang in Thérouanne Cathedral, the items including ' An Anthem of Our Lady and another of St. George '. On October 21 the English monarch embarked from Calais, ' the Chapel Royal being with the Middle Ward '.

Burton, on promise of further preferment, resigned his Keepership of Chestren Wood, Kent, on April 16, 1518, and on May 12 he surrendered a monastic corrody. Two years later, in June 1520, ' Davy ' Burton took part in the magnificent ceremonies of the Field of the Cloth of Gold.

In the list of salaries of the King's household for the year 1526, Burton appears as Gentleman of the Chapel at $7\frac{1}{2}d$. a day, but his name is disguised as ' Avery Burnett '. On February 20 of the same year he was leased valuable lands in Lewisham and Lee, Kent, for sixty years, at the rent of 50*s*. A year later, on April 5, 1527, Burton and a fellow-singer of the Chapel Royal, John Till, were leased the fee farms of the manor of Camberwell and Peckham, at £7 per annum.

Among the entries for the ' King's Bank of Payments for half-yearly wages due at Lady Day ' (March 25), 1529, is that of John Till and David Burton, 70*s*.

David Burton

On October 31, 1538, an amount of twenty marks was granted in survivorship to Burton and another member of the King's Household called Haryngton. In this grant the name is given as 'Avery Burnet', a Gentleman of the King's Chapel, while Haryngton had replaced John Till, then recently deceased.

The dissolution of the monasteries gave an opening to Henry VIII to distribute royal favours among the Court officials, and here we are not surprised that an old servant of the King's Chapel, David Burton, had a lease of monastic lands. From the books of the Court of Augmentations, there is an entry under date of March 16, 1541, in which 'Avery Burnet of the Household' was granted a lease for twenty-one years of the cell of Fenkeloo and St. Oswald's, parish of Durham.

However, Burton was now advanced in years, and not likely to live much longer, and here then is nothing very unusual in the entry among the royal grants of 1542 of a reversionary interest in Burton's Crown lease of February 20, 1526, to Henry Byrd, 'yeoman of the chamber'. In this grant, which is on the Patent Rolls, the composer is correctly described as 'David Burton, Gentleman of the King's Chapel'. The date of the patent is October 25, 1542.

I have not succeeded in tracing the exact date of Burton's death, but it probably occurred at the close of the year 1542 or early in 1543.

III. *William Cornish*

THE career of William Cornish as a dramatist, actor, and pro-
ducer of interludes, pageants, &c., has been admirably dealt with
by Professor Wallace in his *Evolution of the English Drama up to
Shakespeare* (Berlin, 1912). In the present survey his musical
activities and the details of his life will occupy our attention.
The extraordinary blunder of the late Mr. W. H. Husk in making
two individuals out of the one, and of actually contributing
memoirs of the two to Grove's *Dictionary of Music and Musicians*
—in fact the two memoirs appear in the same edition of Grove—
renders it particularly necessary to set forth the actual biographical
data of William Cornish. We have read no doubt of ' the two
single gentlemen rolled into one ', but in the present case we have
to deal with one single gentleman who has been expanded into
two !

William Cornish, probably the son of John Cornish, was born
circa 1468, a contemporary of Newark and Burton. The first
record of him is under date of November 12, 1493, when we
find him as the recipient of 13*s.* 4*d.* ' for a prophecy ', written
for Henry VII—as entered in the *Household Book of Henry VII*,
1491–1505. A short time previously he had been paid a hundred
shillings, as a present from the King ; and on July 13, 1494, he
was granted by the King the keeping of a brewhouse and four
other messuages at Charing Cross—a grant unnoticed by Professor
Wallace. It is quite evident that he must have been a member
of the King's Household from 1492, but it is not till 1496
(September 1) that we meet with an entry implying that he was
a Gentleman of the Chapel Royal. This entry reads : ' Item. to
Cornish of the King's Chapel, 26*s.* 8*d.*' Four months later, on
January 24, 1497, he was given a commission to impress sailors
to go to Scotland.

William Cornish

There was a grand performance at Court on November 18, 1501, to celebrate the marriage of Arthur Prince of Wales to Katherine of Aragon, in which the Gentlemen of the Chapel Royal took part, while the Children of the Chapel appeared as mermaids and 'sang most sweetly and harmoniously' (Harl. MSS. 69). This performance was a pantomime or disguising, and was probably prepared by Newark, assisted by Cornish. A year later he was paid 13s. 4d. 'for setting of a carol upon Christmas Day '.

Evidently Cornish's pen was not sufficiently guarded as a satirical writer, because he was confined in the Fleet Prison in January 1504, for passing a satire on Sir Richard Empson (Stow's *Annales*, 1615). While in prison in July he wrote a poem entitled ' A treatise between Truth and Information ', and was very soon after released.

The Fayrfax MS. (Add. MSS. 31922) contains sixty-three vocal items and forty-nine instrumental—one hundred and twelve in all, and of these thirteen pieces are from the pen of Cornish—amply evidencing his musical powers. The pieces are twelve vocal and one instrumental—the latter being a setting for three instruments —folio 63b. A ' Salve Regina ' for five voices, by him, is among the Harleian MSS. in the British Museum, while an ' Ave Maria ', also for five voices, is in the Library of the Royal College of Music. Other sacred music by Cornish is to be found in the Eton MS., including a ' Stabat Mater ', and at Caius College, Cambridge.

Among his songs in the Fayrfax MS. are ' Ah ! the sighs that come from my heart ', ' Blow thy horn, hunter ', ' Trolly lolly loly lo ', ' While life or breath is in my breast ', ' My love she mourneth for me ', and ' Adieu, courage, adieu '. His song, ' Thou and I and Amyas ', is in the Brit. Mus. MS. 31922. He also composed the music for three of Skelton's songs, namely, ' Manerly Margery Mylk and Ale ', ' Wofully Araid ', and ' Hayde jolly Rutter-Kyn ', as well as ' Pleasure it is ', and ' Concord as Musical ', and probably ' By a bark as I lay '.

Owing to the continued ill-health of William Newark much of the work of training the Children of the Chapel Royal devolved on Cornish, and at length on September 29, 1509, he took over the mastership formally, receiving a Royal Warrant for a gown on June 5, 1510. Between the years 1510–16 Cornish, Crane, and Kite were the principal performers in the Court plays. Of course, the master accompanied Henry VIII with the Chapel Royal, and arranged the musical performance at Thérouanne and Tournai in September 1513. We are given an interesting tribute to the Chapel Royal choir in a letter from Nid. Sagudino to Alf. Foxari, dated May 3, 1515: ' Mass was sung by his Majesty's choir, whose voices were more divine than human ; never heard such counter basses. After dinner was a concert where the writer was desired to play upon the clavichords and organ ; among the audience was a Brescian [Peter Carmelianus] to whom the King gives 300 ducats annually for playing the lute.'

Perhaps the greatest spectacular triumph of Cornish as Master of the Children was at the Field of the Cloth of Gold in June 1520 ; and we have an entry in the King's Book of Payments of the sum of 103s. 4d. paid him ' for the diets of ten children at 2d. a day for 62 days, from 29 May to 22 July '.

Evidently in 1521 Cornish became invalided, but the King continued to favour him, and on August 20, 1523, he was granted the manor of Hylden, Kent, the grant being made in survivorship to ' Wm. Cornish, Jane, his wife, and Henry, his son '. Not long afterwards he died, probably at the end of October. One thing is certain, his will was proved on December 14, 1523.

IV. *William Crane*

ALTHOUGH it is unfortunate that Crane's compositions have been lost, or at least have so far eluded discovery, yet his importance as a contributor to the development of Tudor music-drama and his reconstruction of the Chapel Royal music cannot be overlooked. As deputy to Cornish (whose biography has previously been given) he took part in several music-plays, and early attracted the notice of King Henry VIII. Cornish, Kite, and Crane were then prime favourites with the English monarch, and it is remarkable that Kite, who was Sub-Dean of the Chapel Royal and was also a Prebendary of Lichfield and Chichester, was promoted to the primatial see of Armagh on October 24, 1513, retiring from same in 1521 for the bishopric of Carlisle.

The earliest official appearance of William Crane in Court records is on June 3, 1509, when, as Gentleman of the Chapel Royal, he was appointed by the young King as Water-bailiff of Dartmouth. He took part in the Court Revels of November 14, 1510, and again on February 12 and 13, 1511, in which the King was a performer. On August 18, 1511, he was granted certain tenements in London. On October 6, 1512, he was licensed to export six hundred sacks of wool. In 1512, and again in 1513, he received a loan of £1,000 (a large sum in those days); and in July 1513 he paid £94 7s. 1d. for cables, for the King.

On January 6, 1514, Crane took part in Cornish's Mask of 'The Triumph of Love and Beauty', and he set music for Henry Medwall's Morality, 'The Finding of Truth', which followed the Mask. Professor Wallace, from imperfect knowledge, refers to the author of 'Nature' as 'the impossible Medwell' (*sic*), but it is now agreed that Henry Medwall (not Medwell) was no unworthy precursor of Shakespeare. I may add that the only known copy of his play, 'Fulgens and Lucrese', printed by John Rastall in 1519, was sold by Sotheby in March 1919, for £3,400.

23

Early Tudor Composers

On February 21, 1514, Crane was appointed Comptroller of the Petty Customs in the Port of London. At a Court Play on January 6, 1515, he and Master Harry Stevenson of the Chapel were resplendent in ' plunket satin '. He was also present at the Field of the Cloth of Gold in June 1520 ; and in January 1523 was in the train of Lord Berners, Deputy of Calais.

At length, on March 25, 1523, on the resignation of William Cornish, the coveted position of Master of the Children of the Chapel Royal was given to Crane. This position was materially improved by the Eltham ordinances in January 1526, when the number of boys in the Chapel was increased from ten to twelve, and the salary of the Master augmented from 40 marks to £40. It was also ordered that the Master, with six of the Children and six Gentlemen of the Chapel, ' shall give their continual attendance in the King's Court, and daily to hear a Mass of Our Lady before noon, and on Sundays and Holy Days Mass of the day besides Our Lady Mass, and an *Antempe* in the afternoon '. This early recognition of the anthem as part of the evening service is noteworthy, as it has been frequently stated that anthems were only introduced under Elizabeth. And it must not be forgotten that as early as 1502 Dr. Fayrfax got 20s. from Princess Elizabeth ' for setting of an Anthem '. Anyhow, it is distinctly to the credit of Crane that he increased the number of choirboys in the Chapel Royal, and improved the musical services—with the cordial co-operation of the Dean of the Chapel, Dr. Sampson, who held office from 1523 to 1540, and who was a composer of no mean order.

The following is the official list of the Chapel Royal establishment in 1526, under Crane :

Dean, Richard Sampson, LL.D.	.	.	£33	6	8
Master, William Crane .	.	.	.	26	13	4

Ministers of the Chapel Royal at 7½d. a day :

Ric. Ward, Thos. Hall, Ric. Elys, Ant. Dogget, Thos. Wescot, Emery Tuckfield, Andrew Tracey, Nic. Archbold, William Walker—*Priests*.

William Crane

Robert Pende, John Fisher, Henry Stephenson, Thos. Bury, Wm. Colman, Robert Jones, Robert Phillips, Avery Burton, Hugh Rhodes, Thos. Byrd, Richard Bowyer, Richard Piggot, Edm. Peckham, Robert Perry, Wm. Barber, John Fuller, Robert Richmond, John Aleyn, Richard Stephen—*Gentlemen.*

In the Patent Rolls, under date of May 12, 1526, the grant to William Crane is duly enrolled, and we read that the Master was to be paid ' £40 a year for the instruction, vestures, and beds of twelve boys '. Some months later (January 28, 1527) he was licensed to import 500 tuns of Toulouse woad or Gascon wine. A year afterwards (May 6, 1528) he was appointed to fit out three ships and three galleys for the King. On November 26, 1531, a grant, in fee, was made out in favour of Wm. Crane, *Armiger*, by which he became owner of Beaumont's Inn, parish of St. Michael, Cripplegate, and two other messuages, ' void by the forfeiture of Francis Lovell, late Lord Lovell '.

No previous investigator of the career of Crane has noted that he was commissioned to impress choirboys for the Chapel Royal —a form of conscription that was used as far back as 1420, a fact which I made known for the first time in 1912. The commission to Crane is missing, but I find payment made to him for his expenses in going to the country to procure suitable choristers, in a document dated June 15, 1531—the amount of the expenses being given as £3 6s. 8d.

Crane, like his predecessor Cornish, was a married man, and had a daughter, a fact which we learn from an interesting letter written by the Archbishop of York to Christopher Draper on January 29, 1535, wherein the Archbishop regrets that he cannot give Draper a prebend ' unless he were in orders, at least ton-sured ', but that as Draper ' was insured to Mr. Crane's daughter of the Chapel ' he could not get the promotion.

Further marks of royal favour continued to be poured on Crane, who, on July 2, 1535 (Professor Wallace gives the date as June 28), was made Water-bailiff of Lynn, in Norfolk, *vice* George Lovekin

deceased. His friend Richard Sampson, Dean of the Chapel Royal, was given the post of Coadjutor Dean of St. Paul's Cathedral on February 20, 1536, inasmuch as Dean Pace had become mentally afflicted, and on June 11 he was appointed by Henry VIII as Bishop of Chichester (retaining his Deanery of the Chapel Royal), being dispensed by Archbishop Cranmer (July 20) to hold the Deanery of St. Paul's *in commendam* on the death of Richard Pace —his Deanery of Windsor being given to William Frankelyn.

On January 7, 1538, Master Cranwell paid Mr. Crane 100 marks for Havering Park. Two years later, on March 3, 1540, Crane and his wife Margaret were granted ten tenements and certain rooms at St. Helen's, Bishopsgate. About this time Bishop Sampson did not show sufficient zeal in the cause of the new-fangled doctrines, and in July he was imprisoned, and deprived of his Deanery of the Chapel Royal, which was then given to Thomas Thirlby, newly created Bishop of Westminster, with Richard Wade as Sub-Dean.

On March 6, 1542, Crane was licensed to export 400 tuns of double beer; and on May 2, 1543, he got custody of certain lands. This is the last entry we meet with concerning this many-sided and wealthy Master of the Children of the Chapel Royal, save that he presented the customary Court play in the Carnival period of 1544.

A noteworthy event of Crane's last year was the introduction of the Litany, ' set for five voices, according to the notes used in the King's Chapel', and published by Grafton in October 1544. Crane received his last payment as Master on April 21, 1545, and he fell seriously ill in June, so that on June 30 Richard Bowyer was appointed his successor. He made his will on July 6, and died soon afterwards, being interred in the Church of St. Helen's, Bishopsgate. Although his will was not proved till April 6, 1546, it is tolerably certain that Crane died in September or October 1545, as his successor's appointment was confirmed by Patent dated November 6, 1545.

V. *William Newark*

UP to the present the earliest notices given of William Newark are in 1483 and in 1503-4. In the latter year his name appears among the Gentlemen of the King's Chapel at the funeral of Queen Elizabeth, wife of King Henry VII (*The King's Musick*, by Henry Cart de Lafontaine, 1908). However, this distinguished choirmaster and composer was famous at an earlier period, and eventually succeeded Gilbert Banaster as Master of the Children of the Chapel Royal in 1486.

William Newark was born (? in Newark on Trent) about the year 1450, and displayed uncommon musical ability at an early age. In 1477-8 we find him a Gentleman of the Chapel Royal, and he served as such under Kings Edward IV, Edward V, Richard III, Henry VII, and the first year of Henry VIII. He was evidently in Court favour, as, in 1479, he was granted a corrody in the monastery of St. Mary, Thetford, a substantial gift duly recorded in the Patent Rolls of Richard III, and dated November 28, 1480. Four years later his services were recognized in a more substantial form, and he was given a grant for life of a yearly rent of £20, accruing from the King's manor of Bletchingley, Surrey. This grant was also entered on the Patent Rolls, 2 Rich. III, and bears the date April 6, 1485.

As has been seen in the first chapter of this volume, Gilbert Banaster, Master of the Children of the Chapel Royal, resigned his office on September 29, 1486, but retained three valuable corrodies till his death in the last week of August 1487. One of these corrodies was attached to the monastery of St. Benets Holme, Norfolk, and, on September 1, 1487, King Henry VII granted it to Newark for life. Doubtless this farm was given to Newark as a solatium for not being appointed, as his merits deserved, to succeed Banaster, but certain it is that Laurence Squire (of whose musical abilities nothing has been handed down),

27

Early Tudor Composers

Chaplain to the King, Canon of St. Mary Magdalene, Bridge-north, and Canon of the Collegiate Church of St. Mary, Warwick, was appointed Master of the Children, at a salary of 40 marks a year, on September 29, 1486.

We next meet with an entry of a handsome *douceur* to Newark on New Year's Day 1493, as appears from the Household Book of Henry VII, 1491–1505, under date of January 6, 1493. This payment was the not inconsiderable sum of twenty shillings ' for making of a song ' as a New Year's offering (Brit. Mus. Add. MSS. 7099, folio 7).

Singular to relate, there is no record of any special choir work done by Laurence Squire in the years 1487–93, but he fell ill in the spring of the latter year and died on May 30. Professor Wallace, however, gives us the interesting information (*Evolution of the English Drama up to Shakespeare*, Berlin, Reimer, 1912) that ' the entertainment duties of the Master of the Chapel were first supplemented under Canon Laurence Squire by an Abbot or Lord of Misrule, and that the office of the latter was, in the end, partially absorbed by the Master of the Revels '. Certain it is that, in 1492 and 1495, the provider of the Christmas Revels was known as ' Abbot of Misrule ', and it is equally certain that for the Christmas ' disportes ' of 1490–1, Squire arranged the entertainment given by the children of the Chapel, in which they acted and sang as mermaids.

The last payment due to Squire was paid to William Newark, from which it is evident that the latter had been at once appointed to fill the vacant post of Master of the Children, as his patent was enrolled on September 17, 1493, *durante beneplacito*.

During the Christmas festivities of 1505–6, and again in 1506–7 and 1507–8, Newark had to superintend and devise the musical entertainments at Court. His patent as Master of the Children of the Chapel Royal was renewed under Henry VIII on June 4, 1509, but he fell seriously ill in the early autumn of the same year, and died in November. His will is dated November 5, 1509, and it was proved on December 13 (Rochester Wills, Book 6, folio 262). His body was laid at rest in the porch of Greenwich Church.

William Newark

The titles of Newark's vocal compositions in the Fayrfax volume in the British Museum are as follows : ' The farther I go, the more behind ' (two voices) ; ' What causeth me woful thoughts ? ' (two voices) ; ' So far, I trow, from remedy ' (two voices) ; ' O my desire, what aileth thee ? ' (two voices) ; ' But why am I so abused ? ' (three voices) ; ' Your counterfeiting with double dealing ' (three voices) ; ' Thus musing in my mind ' (three voices).

VI. *Hugh Aston*

It is no small compliment to the cult of early Tudor music to find a brilliant professor of the University of Brussels, M. Charles van den Borren, devoting much attention to the *Sources of Keyboard Music in England*, and publishing the result of his researches in book form, of which an excellent English translation has been made by Mr. James E. Matthew [1]. In the opinion of Van den Borren, Hugh Aston is one of the most considerable figures in the development of virginal music of the early years of the sixteenth century, ' whose importance has not been sufficiently insisted upon by historians of music '. He gives many pages to an analysis of Aston's compositions, but in regard to his biography he is content with the bald statement that he was ' an organist and composer of sacred music of the time of Henry VIII (1509–47) '.

Probably the best account of Hugh Aston is that which is given in the new edition of Grove's *Dictionary of Music and Musicians*, by Mr. Arkwright. The reader may also profitably consult the Carnegie edition. Yet the biographical data—apart from the list of compositions—can only be described as disappointing. Here it is : ' One of the leading English pre-Reformation composers (fl. 1500–20) ; his identity with an ecclesiastic of this name (for whom see the *Dictionary of National Biography*) cannot be proved.' Dr. Ernest Walker, in his *History of Music in England* (1907), says that Mr. Henry Davey's identification of Aston with an Archdeacon of York, who died in 1522, ' is purely conjectural ' ; while Mr. Percy A. Scholes is content with the statement : ' Nothing is known of his life.'

The difficulty over the biography of Hugh Aston is heightened by reason of the name's being spelled variously as Aston, Ashton,

---

[1] Novello (1915).

Hugh Aston

and Assheton, and still more from the fact that two ecclesiastics of the same name were contemporaneous. Mr. Henry Davey (in his useful *History of English Music*) was led astray by the similarity of names, and fell into a pardonable error in assuming that Hugh Aston, Archdeacon of York, was the same man as the composer. Had he investigated the State Papers or the Wills, he would have found that the Archdeacon of York could not have been the same individual as the Hugh Aston of musical fame, for the former was alive in January 1523, whereas the latter was then some months dead.

Hugh Aston was born about the year 1480, and is said to have been a Lancashire man, which is not unlikely. He supplicated for B.Mus. on November 20, 1510—'His Mass and Antiphons are to remain in the hands of the proctors '—described as ' Hugh Assheton, clerk' (*Oxf. Reg.* i. 73). On May 31, 1515, a certain Hugh Aston was appointed Prebendary of York ; but this is not our Hugh Aston.

No further details can be gleaned from official records as to the composer Aston until we reach the year 1522, when, on November 23, is chronicled the death of Hugh Aston, Canon of St. Stephen's, Westminster. This ecclesiastic is the celebrated musician whose biography has hitherto been so elusive. His will was proved in December 1522, a fact which at once destroys his identity with Hugh Aston, of York, because we know that the latter was certainly alive at the close of December 1522, and had been Prebendary of York from May 31, 1515, to January 1523. From the *Calendar of Letters and Papers of Henry VIII* we learn that on January 10, 1523 (Privy Seal dated December 31, 1522), Roger Drew, clerk, was presented to the prebend in St. Stephen's, Westminster, vacant by the death of Hugh Aston.

Among the manuscripts in the British Museum (Royal Appendix 58, ff. 40–9) dating from the first quarter of the sixteenth century are compositions for the virginal or spinet, written on two staves of from five to seven lines, including a ' Hornpipe, by Hugh Aston '. The ascription of ' Hugh Aston's ground ' to our composer is probably to be regarded in the light of an ' arrangement ', because the same theme has been treated by Byrd and by Francis Tregian. In the library of Christ Church, Oxford, there is a composition by William Whytbroke entitled ' Hugh Ashton's Maske ', in four parts, wanting the bass, evidently an elaboration of Aston's theme, whether original or adapted.

It has been surmised that two other virginal compositions in the same Royal Appendix 58, namely, ' Lady Carey's Dumpe '

and ' the short mesure of my Lady Wynkfylde's Round ', are by Hugh Aston, but both are anonymous, and the evidence for such an ascription is not convincing. Stafford Smith, in his *Musice Antique* (1812), ascribes ' My Lady Carey's Dumpe ' to a certain Edmund Spencer. Anyhow, Aston's ' Hornpipe ' is a very real contribution to the virginal music of the period 1500–20, showing a good concept of the variation form with a drone bass. In fact, this little virginal piece, as M. van den Borren says, ' shows the

Hugh Aston

art of variation arrived at a degree of development of which the Continent offers no example '.

As might be expected from a churchman, Aston has left us many interesting specimens of his ability in the domain of ecclesiastical music. Two of his Masses, one for six voices (' Videte manus meas ') and another for five voices (' Te Deum '), are in the Oxford Music School Collection, while there is a fine ' Te Deum ' for five voices by him in the Bodleian Library (e. 1–5). This ' Te Deum ', as my friend Mr. H. B. Collins assures me, is the self-same as ' Te Matrem Dei ' of Cambridge University, St. John's, and the Brit. Mus. Harl. 1709. (In the last named it is attributed to Ashwell.) Many of his motets are to be found in Cambridge, at Peterhouse, at University College, and at St. John's College. His ' Gaude Virgo ' is also to be met with—but in an imperfect state—in the British Museum (Add. MSS. 34191).

However, it is as one of the earliest English composers for the virginal that Hugh Aston deserves to be held in remembrance, although one cannot agree with the fulsome eulogy of entitling him ' the inventor of instrumental composition in Europe '.

VII. *Richard Pygot*

ALTHOUGH Richard Pygot does not loom very large as an actual composer, yet as a trainer of composers and choir-master under Henry VIII he deserves to be held in remembrance. For over thirty years he laboured in the cause of music, and as a favoured Court musician enjoyed unusual preferment. His name figures among the composers of the music printed in that unique work, *Twenty Songs, IX of IIII parts and XI of III parts*, published by Wynkyn de Worde on October 10, 1530, containing compositions by Cornish, Ashwell, Cowper, Fayrfax, Jones, Sturton, Taverner, Gwynneth, and Pygot—of which the only known copy is in the British Museum.

Richard Pygot was born *circa* 1485, and at an early age entered the service of Cardinal Wolsey as a chorister. As early as 1516 we find him as Master of the Children of Wolsey's Chapel, an institution analogous to the Chapel Royal, the singers of which rivalled, if not surpassed, those of Henry VIII's own establishment. On January 27, 1517, he received pardon for infringing the statute *re* crossbows and hand guns. The following extract from a letter by Dean Pace to Wolsey, on March 25, 1518, gives an interesting notice of Pygot's success as a choir-trainer—all the more valuable testimony inasmuch as Dean Pace was an excellent amateur musician who had studied for many years at Rome :

> The King hath plainly shewn unto Cornish [William Cornish, Master of the Boys of the Chapel Royal] that your Grace's Chapel is better than his, and proved the same by this reason that if any manner of new song [melody] should be brought into both the said Chapels [the King's Chapel and Wolsey's Chapel] to be sung *ex improviso* [at sight] then the said song should be better and more surely handled by your Chapel than by his Grace's.

34

Richard Pygot

Pace wrote a further letter on the following day to Wolsey :

> The King has spoken to me again about the child of your Chapel. He is desirous to have it without the procuring of Cornish or other ;

in other words, if Wolsey would not send the boy to the Chapel Royal, Cornish would adopt the expedient of impressment or conscription. As a result, on March 29, Pace informed Wolsey that the King thanked him for the child of his Chapel, 'whom he wouldn't have desired except from necessity', and that he (Pace) 'had spoken to Cornish to treat the child honestly '.

In a fifth letter on the same subject, also from Pace to Wolsey, dated April 1, we note that Cornish was lavish in his praise of the boy of Wolsey's Chapel, 'not only for his sure and cleanly singing but also for his good and crafty discant'. Pace further informs the Cardinal that Cornish also praised Pygot for his excellent method of training : 'Cornish doth in like manner extol Mr. Pygot for the teaching of him.' It may be added that this discriminating musical amateur, who 'discovered' Pygot, was made Dean of St. Paul's Cathedral in succession to Dean Colet, on October 25, 1519.

On January 20, 1520, the King paid a surprise visit, with nineteen gentlemen, to Wolsey's palace of Durham House, where he was royally entertained—Pygot directing the incidental music. Four years later, in 1524, Pygot was appointed a Gentleman of the Chapel Royal, but retained his post in Wolsey's Chapel till the fall of the great Cardinal in 1529. It would seem that he was Deputy Master of the Children of the Chapel Royal in 1526, and we find a pension paid to him as such on May 1, 1527, ' the pension payable by the Abbot-elect of Whitby '.

Pygot retained the royal favour after Wolsey's death, and on October 7, 1532, he was given a corrody in the monastery of Coggeshall, Essex, surrendered by William Colman. Further preferment awaited him, as on May 12, 1533, there is an entry in the Patent Rolls of his presentation to the canonry and prebend of Tamworth, *vice* Thomas Wescote, resigned.

Early Tudor Composers

Notwithstanding the suppression of the monastery of Coggeshall, an order was made on February 5, 1538, that ' Pygot of the Chapel ' was to be paid his pension out of the confiscated property. Pygot also had a corrody out of the Abbey of Tower Hill, as by an order of March 23, 1538, Sir Thomas Seymour was bound to pay him a pension of £4 10s. His name appears in the royal pensions list regularly during 1540-7.

On October 31, 1541, Richard Pygot was given a substantial sum for his house at Greenwich. But he must have continued to reside in the same locality, for on September 29, 1543, his name appears in the annuity list as ' of East Greenwich '.

Owing to some informality—very likely because he was a layman, and not even in minor orders—Pygot resigned his canonry and prebend of Wylmecot in Tamworth Collegiate Church of St. Edith ; but on October 13, 1545, he was again presented to it by royal favour. In the following month a royal letter was written to the Dean and Chapter of Wells ' to suffer Richard Pygot of the Chapel to reside upon his prebend there, *notwithstanding his laity*'. Pygot composed a lovely carol for four voices, ' Quid petis, O Fili'. He composed a Mass, ' Veni Sancte Spiritus ' (Peterhouse and Add. 34191, f. 4b), and two motets, ' Gaude pastore ' (Add. 34191, f. 23) and ' Salve Regina ' (Harley, 1709, f. 26).

The last payment of £6 13s. 4d. a quarter by Henry VIII to Richard Pygot was made on October 2, 1546, and in the account of liveries given out for the funeral of the English monarch on February 16, 1547, his name appears among the ' Gentlemen of the Chapel Royal '.

Pygot's services were retained by Edward VI, and he was in high favour at Court. On December 19, 1551, he was given the sum of 30s. by the Princess Elizabeth, who also presented him with a *douceur* of 21s. on January 12, 1552. This is the last reference I have met with regarding the career of Richard Pygot, and he probably died in 1552.

VIII. *Robert Fayrfax*

THE best available account of the compositions of Fayrfax is that contributed by Mr. Godfrey E. P. Arkwright to the new edition of *Grove*; yet Fayrfax's biography has been somewhat inadequately told. There is a good conspectus of Fayrfax's works and an account of his technique in the Historical Survey which forms the preface to *Tudor Church Music*, vol. i. None of our musical historians have penetrated his career prior to the year 1502, when he is met with at St. Albans, being then a Doctor of Music of Cambridge University. Anthony Wood says that Fayrfax was organist or Informator Chori of the Abbey of St. Albans in 1502, and that in his day he was ' in great renown and accounted the prime musician of the nation '. Probably the former statement rests on the entry under date March 28, 1502, in the Privy Purse Expenses of Queen Elizabeth of York, from which it appears that he received at St. Albans the sum of twenty shillings ' for setting an Anthem of Our Lady and St. Elizabeth ', probably his ' Aeterne laudis lilium '. Yet from two entries in the recently published *Calendar of Patent Rolls of Henry VII*, 1494–1509, it is probable that Fayrfax was a Gentleman of the Chapel Royal in 1496, and possibly earlier.

Bishop Tanner says that this remarkable English musician was born at Bayford, in Hertfordshire, and this event may be placed as *circa* 1465 or 1466. He may have been a boy chorister in the Chapel Royal in 1480, but one thing is certain, he was a Gentleman of the King's Chapel in 1496.[1] The fact of occupying this post may be taken as evidence of his musical skill in the last decade of the fifteenth century, and he probably studied under

---

[1] According to Venn's *Alumni Cantabrigienses* (1922), Robert Fayrfax was of Acaster Malbis, Yorks., the fourth son of Sir Thomas Fayrfax of Walton, and graduated Mus. Bac. of Cambridge in 1500-1. (Vol. ii, p. 117.)

Early Tudor Composers

Gilbert Banaster (1478–86), Laurence Squire (1486–93), and William Newark (1493–1509), who were in succession Masters of the Children of the Chapel Royal. Anyhow, in 1497 he was granted the free chapel of Snodhill in Herefordshire. The entry runs as follows : 1497, December 7, ' Grant to Robert Fayrfax, one of the Gentlemen of the King's Chapel, of the free chapel in the Castle of Snodhill, in the diocese of Hereford, void by the death of Master Richard Jackson.'

Less than a year later, on November 16, 1498, another entry supplies the information that Fayrfax had resigned the chapelry, which was then given to Robert Cowper. It is very probable that he surrendered this ecclesiastical benefice in order to take up the post of organist at St. Albans Abbey, and if so, this occurred at the Christmastide of 1498.

As has been stated, Fayrfax was at St. Albans in 1502, and, doubtless, from St. Albans came the suggestion of the Albanus Mass, but evidently he must have returned to London before the accession of King Henry VIII. He supplicated for the Mus.D. of Cambridge in 1502, and was granted it in 1504, his exercise being the five-part Mass, ' O quam glorifica ' (*Oxf. Reg.* i. 78). A portion of his song, ' Somewhat musing ', was discovered in the binding of a book in Wells Library. His name appears in the list of the Chapel Royal at the funeral of Queen Elizabeth of York on February 23, 1503, and again at the funeral of King Henry VII in April 1509. Two months later, on June 22, the new King, Henry VIII, granted him (with another) an annuity of £9 2s. 6d., and his name appears at the head of the singing men at the King's coronation. In December 1510 he was paid £7 17s. 4d. for the board and education of two of the Chapel Royal boys, William Alderson and Arthur Lovekin, the King's scholars. The name of ' Mr. Doctor Fayrfax ' appears at the head of the Chapel Royal singers at the funeral of Prince Henry, on February 22, 1511. In 1511, Robert Fayrfax, D.Mus. Camb., supplicated for incorporation at Oxford. His motet, ' Ave Dei Patris ' for five voices is in Christ Church Library, Oxford. His madrigal, ' I love, loved, and loved would I be ', was printed by the Plain Song and Medieval

38

Music Society (1891). He surrendered a corrody in Stanley Monastery in 1513, which was given to John Fisher, Gentleman of the Chapel Royal (March 6, 1513). A new patent was made out for his annuity of £9 2s. 6d. on November 16, 1513; and, in December, he got 104 shillings for the two King's scholars.

Dr. Fayrfax must have been in high favour at Court, because, on September 10, 1514, he was appointed 'one of the poor knights of Windsor with 12d. a day'. On January 1, 1516, he was paid the large sum of £13 6s. 8d. for a book; on New Year's Day of the following year he got £20 'for a Book of Anthems'; on January 1, 1518, he was given £10 'for a prick-song book'; and on January 1, 1519, a similar sum 'for a balet-boke limned'. One of these four books is supposed, with good reason, to be the celebrated Fayrfax MS.

In the List of the Chapel at the Field of the Cloth of Gold in June 1520, Fayrfax stands at the head of the Singing Men. This was his last public appearance. Mr. Arkwright cautiously states that his death 'probably took place before January 1, 1525/6', but the actual date was Thursday, October 24, 1521. He desired to be buried at St. Albans, and was interred in the presbytery of the Abbey, where a fine brass—long since disappeared—to the memory of Robert Fayrfax and Agnes, his wife, and their children was erected. His wife, Agnes, must have survived him, as letters of administration were granted to her on November 14.[1] The following is the wording on the sketch of the brass (made in 1643) which is in the Presbytery of the Abbey Church: 'Pray for the soules of Master Robert Ffayrefax, Doctor of Music, and Agnes his wife and her children. Robert deceased the xxiii. day of October in the year of Our Lord God, mdxxi., on whose soules Jesus have mercy. Amen.'

[1] Venn says that Fayrfax died in 1529. "Will (Archd. St. Albans) 1529".

Library of

Davidson College

IX. *John Browne*

JOHN BROWNE was a not inconsiderable figure in English musical art during the closing years of the reign of Henry VII, and yet scanty details are available as to his biography; in fact, Mr. Barclay Squire says that ' nothing is known of him '. Some writers allege that he flourished in the early portion of Henry VIII's reign, while others place him as ' *circa* 1525 '. His works are fairly numerous, and the British Museum can boast of over a dozen of his compositions. He is represented in the famous Eton College Anthem Book [1] by a six-part ' Stabat Mater ', a five-part ' O Mater venerabilis ', an eight-part ' O Maria salvatoris mater ', a six-part motet ' O Regina mundi clare ', and a five-part ' Salve Regina '. Dr. Ernest Walker, in his admirable *History of Music in England* (1907), quotes with approval John Browne's ' Margaret meeke ', which he describes as written ' in a regular rondo form '.[2]

There has been much confusion over the period of Browne's activity, and this is heightened by the fact that there were two composers of this surname almost contemporaneous. However, their Christian names were not the same, as William Browne of the Chapel Royal was a very different person from John Browne the composer now under notice ; and, moreover, John Browne was dead fully ten years before the accession of Henry VIII, whereas William Browne was alive in 1516.

So far I have not been able to locate the early career of John Browne, but he appears to have been Rector of the Parish Church of West Tilbury in 1480. This post he held till the year 1490,

---

[1] An excellent account of this manuscript, by Mr. Barclay Squire, appears in *Archaeologia*, lvi. Mr. Squire, however, gives a six-part motet, ' O Marie plena gracie ', but this is by Walter Lambe (Dr. James's catalogue).

[2] This madrigal is in the British Museum (Add. MS. 5465).

John Browne

when he resigned. From the printed Calendar of Patent Rolls of Henry VII we learn that on July 20, 1490, Thomas Clerk, chaplain, was presented to the Parish Church of West Tilbury, in the diocese of London, void by the resignation of Master John Browne.

The reason of Master John Browne's resignation was very natural, inasmuch as he had been offered a vacant stall in St. Stephen's Chapel, Westminster. This offer was gratifying, inasmuch as the preferment gave him an opportunity for exercising his musical gifts in the Royal Chapel. He had already been in high favour in Court circles, and on July 29, 1489, there is an entry in the Patent Rolls which informs us that John, Archbishop of Canterbury, legate of the Apostolic See, John Browne, clerk, and Thomas Butler were granted the collation of the next void canonry and prebend in the Chapel of St. Stephen, in the Palace of Westminster. Three years later an Italian musical cleric, Peter Carmelianus, of Brescia, was also admitted to a canonry and prebend in the Collegiate Chapel of St. Stephen.

No other biographical data can be gleaned of this early Tudor composer save of his death, which occurred early in February, 1498. The official reference in the printed Calendar places on record that on February 19, 1498, Stephen Berworth, one of the King's chaplains, was appointed to a prebend in the Collegiate Chapel of St. Stephen, in the Palace of Westminster, void by the death of John Browne.

Thus it is certain that John Browne, the composer, flourished in the reigns of Edward IV, Edward V, Richard III, and Henry VII, and was contemporary with Hothby, Lambe, Abyngdon, Banaster, Pasche, Davy, Aleyn, Gervays, Forest, Cooke, Fayrfax, Newark, and others.

If Browne composed nothing but the charming five-part ' O Mater Venerabilis ', in the Eton MS., ' Wofully arayed ', for four voices, and ' Jesu, mercy, how may this be ? ' for four voices, in the Brit. Mus. MS. 5465, his fame as an early Tudor composer would be sufficiently evidenced. Indeed, the technique is much in advance of the writers at the close of the fifteenth century.

Early Tudor Composers

Others of his ' Madrigals ' are very interesting, notably ' That godly lass ', ' Her lusty cheer ', and ' My Margaret '.

Regarding his early career, Mr. W. Barclay Squire suggests that he may have been the John Browne, of County Bucks, who was admitted at King's College, Cambridge, aged nineteen, in 1445. And this surmise is not unlikely ; but as to the actual facts, the only data at present available are those here presented for the first time.

X. Richard Hygons

THOSE who have studied the famous Eton College MS.—which has been so admirably and minutely described by Mr. W. Barclay Squire in *Archaeologia*, vol. lvi [1]—have been struck with the beauty of the five-part anthem, ' Salve Regina ', by R. Hygons. Yet no details have hitherto appeared as to the biography of Hygons, and the only fact deducible from the MS. is that he lived before the year 1510 or 1515.

As will appear from the succeeding chapter on Richard Bramston, there is mention of Hygons in Mr. John E. West's *Cathedral Organists* (Novello, 1921), as the first recorded organist of Wells Cathedral, under the slightly disguised form of ' Richard Hugo '. Mr. West, however, did not suspect the identity of this ' Hugo ' with Hygons, but the *Calendar of the Manuscripts of the Dean and Chapter of Wells*, vol. ii, issued by the Historical Manuscripts Commission in 1914, leaves no room for doubt, and furnishes unimpeachable material for a memoir of this early Tudor composer.

An antiquarian friend suggested to me that probably Richard Hygons was identical with Richard Huchins, who was a vicar-choral of Wells in 1470 ; but this suggestion cannot stand, because the latter was dead in 1494, and Hygons was certainly living in 1507, as will be seen later. Moreover, the surnames are not the same.

Richard Hygons studied under Abyngdon, and was Master of the Choristers of Wells Cathedral in 1474. In the Chapter Act Book for 1486–7, under date of May 2, 1487, there is a record of a grant to Richard Hygons, Master of the Choristers, ' for his life ', in recognition of ' his diligence and good service ', of an increased salary of 26s. 8d. yearly, issuing from a vacant stall.

[1] See also an article on Eton College by Mr. F. G. Edwards in the *Musical Times* for December, 1908.

Hygons was also organist of Wells Cathedral, and in the Chapter Acts there are several references to the organ and the choristers in the closing years of the fifteenth century[1]. We also learn that Robert Wydow, Mus.Bac., was installed a canon of Wells on September 10, 1497, and was appointed succentor, being further admitted a canon residentiary on February 26, 1499–1500.

Evidently the organist and Master of the Choristers of Wells felt the burden of years in 1507, because on July 23 of that year the Chapter issued an order confirming a private arrangement whereby Richard Bramston was to take over the duties hitherto performed by Hygons, receiving 5s. for the half-quarter ending on September 29 ensuing, and 40s. a year henceforth; the said Bramston undertaking to teach the choristers and also ' to keep and play the organs both in the great choir and the chapel of the Blessed Virgin Mary '.

This arrangement of Bramston as deputy did not last quite a year, as on May 15, 1508, the Chapter appointed John Clausy to the office of Master of the Choristers, ' to instruct them to sing plainchant and discant '. By a strange slip the editor of the *Calendar* (Mr. William Paley Baildon) translates ' ad cantandum et discantandum ' as ' to sing, and sing earnestly ', whereas the ordinary meaning of *discantandum* is ' discant ', in opposition to ' plain chant ', and not to ' sing earnestly '. It is also found as ' in torto cantu ', and has been anglicized ' diffuse chant ' and ' curious singing ' in documents of the mid-sixteenth century. In this Chapter Act, John Clausy is ordered not only to teach the choristers, but also to play the organ ' both in the great choir and in the chapel of the Blessed Virgin Mary behind the high altar *as Richard Hygons did heretofore* '. Further, the said Clausy was to receive four marks from the Clerk of Works of the Cathedral from two vacant stalls, and ' he shall also receive from the escheator all escheats, with the consent of the vicars, *so that the vicars non-perpetuated shall have during the life of Richard*

---

[1] In the Chapter Accounts for 1492–3, a sum of 6s. 8d. was paid to the King's Commissioner ' not to take away three choristers '.

Richard Hygons

Hygons the things which yearly accrue. Moreover, he shall have a house of the yearly value of 26*s.* 8*d.*'

From the same Chapter Act we learn that Richard Hygons, late Master of the Choristers, ' had agreed to pay John Clausy *out of his fee and portion* 40*s.* a year ', with the proviso that ' after Hygons's death, Clausy shall receive *all the fees that Hygons now has* '.

By a strange irony of fate both Hygons and Clausy died early in the year following the above agreement, for under the heading of Receipts in the ' Accounts of Thomas Weston, the Escheator, from Michaelmas, 1508, to Michaelmas, 1509 ', there is a significant entry : ' Oblations : At the anniversary of John Clausy $1\frac{1}{2}d.$; of Mr. John Hanse, $\frac{1}{2}d.$' ; that is to say, the sum of three-halfpence was given as an offering at the burial of John Clausy, and one halfpenny at the burial of Master John Hans, sub-Dean of Wells. The exact date of the death of Hygons is not recorded, but it was probably about the same time as that of the sub-Dean, either in January or February 1509. Certain it is that Hans was replaced as sub-Dean on February 8, 1509, by Reginald West, while John Gye, vicar-choral, appears as organist and choirmaster in 1511, and evidently had been acting as such for some time, as on October 25, 1512, he was given a substantial *douceur* ' for his good and diligent service to God and St. Andrew, namely, *his praiseworthy organ playing* and diligent instruction of the boys and choristers '. I take the liberty of thus translating the italicised words, ' his praiseworthy organ playing ', as more correct than Mr. W. Paley Baildon's reading : ' his musical praises ' ; for the Latin text is distinctly ' laudibus organicis '—literally ' praises on the organ '.

XI. _Richard Bramston_

Just as in the case of Thomas Farthing, whose name was included in Morley's Valhalla of sixteenth-century English composers, so also in the case of Richard Bramston, praised by Morley in his _Plaine and Easie Introduction to Practicall Musicke_ in 1597, we have had no exact biographical data hitherto. ' Master Bramston ', so far as English musical historians are concerned, has remained a ghost-like figure, of whom nothing has been chronicled by Burney, Hawkins, Chappell, Davey, or Grove, save an incidental reference to some of his compositions. Even Mr. Cecil Forsyth, in the chapter on ' The Golden Age ' in the recent _History of Music_ by Sir Charles Stanford and himself (1916), merely includes the name of Bramston in a foot-note as an English composer whose works are to be met with in manuscript. But though many of Bramston's compositions have disappeared, the few that remain give ample evidence of his abilities as a polyphonic composer. Dr. Ernest Walker says that his works deserve mention, yet from a cursory examination I would be inclined to place Bramston's motet, ' Recordare, Domine, testamenti ', as evidencing potential powers quite equal to those of Taverner, Redford, Cowper, or Johnson. In this manuscript, which will be found among the Add. MSS. 17802–17805 of the British Museum, his name appears as ' Master Bramston '. Another beautiful motet, ' Mariae Virgini ', is in Peterhouse College, Cambridge [1].

It is only fair to state that a brief reference to Bramston is given by Mr. John E. West in his excellent book on _Cathedral Organists_ (Novello, 1921), under date of 1507, when he was appointed deputy-organist of Wells Cathedral in place of ' Richard Hugo '.

---

[1] See the Rev. Dr. Jebb's catalogue in the _Ecclesiologist_ for 1859.

46

Richard Bramston

Of Richard Bramston's birth and education there is no evidence forthcoming, but he was a chorister of Wells Cathedral under Henry Abyndon, Robert Wydow, Mus.Bac., and Richard Hygons, between the years 1485 and 1500. Wells at this time was distinguished for its musical traditions, traditions that were carefully fostered by Wydow (who was sub-Dean), Thomas Cornish, *Episcopus Tinensis* (the precentor), and Hugh Inge (succentor), in 1500–7. The choirboys were so good that two of them were impressed for the Chapel Royal, and in the account book of William Capron, who was Communar from 1504 to 1505, there is an entry of ten shillings paid to the royal commissioner who had come ' to take choristers for the King's chapel '.

On January 23, 1507, as appears from the Chapter Acts, Richard Bramston was admitted, on probation, as a vicar-choral of Wells. Six months later, on July 23, he undertook to deputize as organist for Richard Hygons, for which he was to be paid 5*s.* for the half-quarter at Michaelmas, and from that day at the rate of ' 40*s.* a year '. He was also employed to teach the choristers. It appears from the Chapter Acts that Bramston was not only to play the organ ' in the great choir and the chapel of the Blessed Virgin Mary ', but had to act as ' keeper of the organs '.

So highly esteemed were the services of Bramston as temporary organist and master of the choristers, that the Chapter unanimously voted for his retention as vicar-choral in perpetuity, or ' perpetual vicar ', provided that he was diligent in pursuing his musical studies during the following year. This appointment is dated January 25, 1508. It is of interest to note that another vicar who had been on probation was not given the post of perpetual vicar, because it had been testified by John Aleyn and fourteen other vicars-choral that ' he had not a competent voice and was of evil conversation '.

Bramston resigned his post as deputy-organist in May 1508, and was succeeded by John Clausy, who graduated Mus.Bac. at Oxford in the following year. Naturally, Bramston preferred his assured Vicar-choralship, and with a view to qualifying for same, he studied for sub-deaconship. This we learn from a Chapter

47

Act dated September 4, 1509, in which Bramston was warned that he must take sub-deacon's orders before the ensuing Christmas, ' on pain of privation '.

On February 16, 1510, a letter was written to two canons of Wells to petition King Henry VIII against the not infrequent practice of taking up the Wells choristers, and citing the recent case of Richard Bramston, who had lately taken away ' one of our best queresters, that is to say, Farr '; also to petition the King that the Wells Chapter might have permission to impress any boys in monastic or other churches in the diocese to serve Wells Cathedral choir.

Unfortunately there is a lacuna in the Chapter Acts from 1513 to 1534, but there is preserved a charter of the year 1530–1, in which Richard Bramston, vicar-choral, had ' leave of absence from Matins during his lifetime, and two months' leave in each year ', and was confirmed in his ' annuity of 7*d*. a week as Clerk of Works of the Cathedral Church '. On the same day (January 31, 1530–1) he was granted by the Dean and Chapter of Wells an annuity of £4 in consideration of surrendering his office as Clerk of Works, and ' of his surrender of the office of Master of the Choristers, for which he was paid 26*s*. 8*d*. a year '. Both of these interesting documents are signed by ' Ryc. Bramston ', and sealed with his seal, ' a girl's head in profile, to the dexter ' (*MSS. of the Dean and Chapter of Wells*, vol. ii, p. 701).

Bramston's successor as Master of the Choristers was John Smith, jun., in 1536. Nevertheless, the composer was somewhat of a pluralist, because owing to the favour of Thomas Lord Cromwell he was a prebendary of the College of Crediton, and duly received a pension after the dissolution of 40*s*. annually from 1540. He was still alive in 1550, as in the Expenses of the Cathedral from 1549–1550, furnished by himself as ' Keeper of the Fabric ', he received £4 for his annual fee. In this account his surname is given as ' Brampston '.

XII. *John Taverner*

THE fullest account of Taverner is in the first volume of *Tudor Church Music* (Carnegie edition), while a list of his printed and manuscript compositions will be found in the second edition of Grove's *Dictionary of Music and Musicians*. This list includes eight Masses, numerous Latin Services and Motets, various In Nomines, and some English part-songs—overwhelming evidence of Taverner's activity. Until the appearance of *Tudor Church Music* the biographical data may be described as meagre, but some crumbs have fallen to my investigations which may serve to lead students to study Taverner's actual works, in vol. i and vol. ii of *Tudor Church Music*.

John Taverner was almost certainly a native of Lincolnshire (Tattershall or Boston), and was born *circa* 1495. This date is more likely to be correct than ' 1500 ', because Taverner was already a composer of fame in 1521. He was a boy chorister at Tattershall Collegiate Church (founded by Sir Ralph Cromwell, in 1439, for seven priests, six clerks, and six choristers), and had a good master in John Gygur, who was Warden from 1478 to 1500, and was owner of Sloane MS. 1210, from whom it passed to Dom William Stokes, O.S.B.

In 1524 we find Taverner as Master of the Choristers and Stipendiary of Tattershall, and in 1525-6 he was appointed first musical director of Cardinal Wolsey's College at Oxford. On October 17, John Longland, Bishop of Lincoln, wrote to Wolsey that he had sent for ' Taverner, a singing man, to be Informator of the Children of Wolsey's Chapel in his college at Oxford, but cannot induce him to give up his living at Tattershall and the prospect of a good marriage which he would lose by removal '. Bishop Longland suggests to Wolsey that the man to be appointed should have ' both his breast at will [that is, have a good chest voice], the handling of an instrument [organist], pleasure, cunning, and exercise in teaching, and to be there four or five days before your appointed day [of formally opening the College Chapel] for the ordering of the children, and to be acquainted with such songs as shall be the day of solemnity there sung'. He also recommends Wolsey to procure ' Rectors' Staves ' [conductors' batons] and a ' good pair of organs : less than two pair will not do '.

After some parleying, John Taverner consented to take the post at Oxford, and entered on his duties in November 1526, at a salary of £10 a year, with livery and commons. John Higden was Dean of Cardinal College, and on February 24, 1528, he wrote to Wolsey's chaplain that new statutes should be framed for the choir owing to the negligence of some of the ministers of the Chapel, and that fines of 1*d*. and 2*d*. should be inflicted for absence from Matins, Prime, High Mass, Evensong, Compline, and Processions.

In February 1528, owing to the dissemination of heretical books, several students were imprisoned, including Garret, Clarke, Fryer, Fryth, Dyott, and Delaber. Foxe gives a wrong list, and states that Taverner was also ' imprisoned in a deep cave under the ground ', but he afterwards mentions that the Cardinal excused Taverner, ' saying that he was but a musician, and so he escaped '. Dean Higden, in his letter of March 1528, tells Wolsey that he has not committed to prison Taverner or Radley, because ' they were not to be regarded ', and the worst charges against Taverner were ' hiding Mr. Clarke's books, and being privy to the letter sent to him by Garret after his flight '. A month later (April 2) Thomas Cromwell writes to Wolsey that ' his College chapel at Oxford is most devoutly and virtuously ordered : the daily service is solemn and full of harmony '. As against Foxe's account of Fryer's harsh treatment, it is pleasant to quote Fryer's own letter to Wolsey, dated September 16, thanking the Cardinal for having released him ' from that destruction occasioned by his own folly '.

Taverner resigned his post as Director of the Choir at Cardinal College in April 1530, and was paid £5, being his half-yearly salary to March 25. On May 20 Dean Higden engaged the services of John Benbow, from Manchester, as successor of Taverner, who evidently had found a better post, and doubtless had followed the rising star of Master Thomas Cromwell. His contributions to Wynkyn de Worde's *Song Book*, published on October 10, 1530, are three, namely, ' The bella ' (four parts), ' My heart, my mind ', and ' Love will I ' (three parts). About 1530 Taverner composed a Motet, ' O Christi Jesu ', containing a prayer for Henry VIII. This prayer was afterwards changed to one for Queen Elizabeth in 1560.

One of Taverner's friends, John Wendon, Mus.Bac., organist of Boston Parish Church, sent Cromwell a present of ' a fat swan and a fat crane ' on January 8, 1535. Taverner himself secured a lucrative ' job ' from Cromwell, and was appointed with another time-server called Jones to arrange matters for the suppression of the four friaries at Boston in August 1538. Richard Ingworth, Bishop of Dover (an official receiver of the suppressed houses), wrote to Cromwell under date of February 2, 1539, that ' he received to the King's use the four friary houses in Boston, and gave them to Taverner and Jones '. Previous to this he had married Rose Parrowe of Spalding—who survived to May 1553. On May 2, 1540, he wrote to Cromwell on behalf of a relative. Less than two months later, on June 28, Cromwell was executed on Tower Hill, ' unwept and unpitied ', as Cardinal Gasquet writes. He was a member of the Guild of Corpus Christi from 1537 to 1543, and was steward 1541–3. According to Baldwin's MS. (Ch. Ch., Oxford, 983 f. 46), ' he died at Boston, and there lieth ', probably in 1548.[1]

---

[1] As the Bodleian Mus. School MS. e. 420–422, in Taverner's handwriting, is regarded as dating from 1548, Taverner must have been alive at that date.

XIII. *Thomas Farthing*

In the valuable list of old English composers printed by Morley, in 1597, as an Addendum to his *Plaine and Easie Introduction to Practicall Musicke*, appears the name of Farthing. Many specimens of Farthing's powers as a composer have survived, and one of them, ' In May, that lusty season ', is quoted by Dr. Ernest Walker in his *History of Music in England* (1907). Yet, strange to say, up to the present no musical historian has attempted to lift the veil which hid the identity of this early Tudor composer. Not even a fairly approximate date has been furnished for the period of his musical activities, save merely a haphazard statement that he probably flourished ' under Henry VII and Henry VIII '—a period of sixty-two years—rather vague, indeed. As to his personality not a hint has previously been given. Hence it is with special pleasure I present the following definite information regarding the composer of ' The thought within my breast ', ' With sorrowful eyes ', ' I love truly ', and a nameless three-part piece. The three last named are in the British Museum (Add. MS. 31922).

Thomas Farthing (the name is variously written Farding and Farthyng) was born *circa* 1475, and in 1508 we first meet with him as a singer in the chapel of the Countess of Richmond and Derby, the mother of King Henry VII. On the decease of this noble and philanthropic lady we find that she bequeathed annuities to her retainers, including Hugh Aston, Thomas Farthing, and others. Late in the following year (1509) Farthing was given a post as Gentleman of the Chapel Royal under William Cornish ; and his name appears among those who received mourning livery for the funeral of Prince Henry, who died on February 22, 1511. On July 8, 1511, Thomas Farthing had confirmation from

52

Thomas Farthing

King Henry VIII of the annuity of ten marks which had been bequeathed to him by the Countess of Richmond and Derby, and in this document (printed in the *Calendar of Letters and Papers of Henry VIII*) his name appears as 'Thomas Farding, Gentleman of the King's Chapel'. He took part in the various Masques and Disguisings played at Court during the years 1511 and 1512, and he accompanied King Henry VIII to France in June 1513, as one of the Chapel Royal, taking part in the magnificent choral services at Thérouanne, Lille, and Tournai in September of that year. Warrants for gowns to him were issued in 1513–14.

The name of Thomas Farthing appears as a singing-man among the list of the Gentlemen of the Chapel Royal who took part in the gorgeous pageants at the Field of the Cloth of Gold, in June 1520, along with William Cornish as Master of the Choristers, and Dr. John Clerk as Dean of the Chapel Royal. Farthing's friend, Dr. Richard Pace, Dean of St. Paul's Cathedral, preached a Latin oration on this memorable occasion at the Val Doré, ever since known as 'Champ du Drap d'Or'.

In recognition of Farthing's services as a composer and singer, King Henry VIII granted him a fine mansion house at East Greenwich on condition of a fine to the outgoing tenant, Thomas Ritter. The date of the grant is November 21, 1520, and the précis of the document is as follows :

> 1520. 21 Nov. Grant to Thomas Fardyng, Gentleman of the Chapel Royal, and his heirs for ever, by the service of a red rose, if it be asked, of a Tenement in East Greenwich, formerly in the tenure of Robert Johns, and lately of Thomas Ritter, gent. usher of the Chamber, who has compounded with Fardyng.

We next find a notice of Farthing as having taken part in the Revels at Greenwich on December 9, 1520, an entertainment at which John Heywood also assisted ; but it was Farthing's last appearance in public. Three days later he was seized with illness, and his death occurred quite suddenly on December 12, 1520, at his house at East Greenwich.

53

Early Tudor Composers

It is of interest to note that the annuity of ten marks which Farthing had enjoyed from 1509 to 1520 was allotted to another Court musician, John Heywood, named above, then rising in favour. The official grant was dated February 4, 1521, and the Letters Patent may be summarized as follows : ' John Heywood, the King's servant, is to have the annuity of ten marks, as held by Thomas Farthing, deceased.'

No doubt many of the compositions of Farthing are regarded as crude, but there is a good vein of melody running through them, and it must be remembered that his creative period was between the years 1500 and 1518. Although he cannot be rated as highly as his contemporary, Fayrfax, who died in October 1521, it is, of course, probable that much of the music by Farthing—now, alas ! lost or undiscovered—may have contained beauties equal to those of Fayrfax, Browne, Dygon, Chard, Pygot, Ashwell, Hyllary, Davy, Alcock, Jones, and Whytbroke. Yet this is but speculation. As for his biography, the only known facts are those contained in the present chapter, mainly based on the monumental *Calendar of Letters and Papers of Henry VIII.*

XIV. *Thomas Ashwell*

As a brilliant contemporary of Fayrfax it is surprising that the work of Thomas Ashwell has not received adequate recognition long ere this. Notwithstanding the destruction of manuscripts at the period of the so-called Reformation, quite a respectable number of Masses, Motets, songs, &c., by Ashwell may be cited as proof of his powers. In particular, he was one of the first—if not actually the first—among English composers to give us a setting of the ' Stabat Mater'. Of course, we know that Fayrfax did compose a setting of this beautiful Sequence, which was formerly included in the well-known Eton MS.; but, alas! the pages containing it are long since missing. On this account, Ashwell's setting is of unique interest. There are settings of the ' Stabat Mater' by Davy and Browne complete in the Eton MS., and a setting by Cornish.

Yet another claim to fame may be put forward in the case of Thomas Ashwell, namely, that he composed a royal anthem, ' God save King Herry ', which may be regarded as the precursor of the present National Anthem. The date of this English Anthem—composed for the marriage of Henry VII to Elizabeth of York—can be fixed with tolerable certainty, for the nuptials took place on January 17, 1485/6. And a third claim to notoriety is the inclusion of a song by Ashwell in Wynkyn de Worde's printed Song Book of 1530, in which he is represented by a four-part setting of ' She may be called a soverant lady'. Yet the strange circumstance is that no memoir of this remarkable musician has yet appeared, nor have any facts of his career been hitherto published. All that has emerged is that Ashwell lived ' between the years 1485 and 1510 ', and that he is included by Morley in his list of famous English musicians of the early sixteenth century.

Early Tudor Composers

For a long time I believed that Ashwell held a Court appointment under Henry VII, or else that he was in some way connected with the Chapel Royal, but after a protracted search I found that such a claim was groundless. Nor does his name occur in the monumental *Calendar of Letters of Henry VIII*. However, I was fortunate to locate him as Master of the Choristers of Lincoln Cathedral in 1508.

It is to be regretted that the published *Chapter Acts of Lincoln Cathedral*, carefully edited by Canon R. E. G. Coles, in three volumes, for the Lincoln Record Society, begins only in 1520, and consequently gives no information about Thomas Ashwell. Yet a reference to the late Canon Maddison's excellent little book on the *Vicars-choral, Poor Clerks, and Organists of Lincoln Cathedral, from the Twelfth Century to the Accession of Edward VI*, printed privately in 1878, confirms the statement that Thomas Ashwell was appointed Master of the Choristers—evidently in succession to John Davy—in 1508. At the same date Leonard Peper, a vicar-choral, was acting as organist, ' ad lusus organorum in alto choro '.

Yet though Ashwell was Master of the Choristers of Lincoln in 1508, he was not a vicar-choral, nor a chorister, nor a Poor Clerk of that Cathedral, and does not seem to have been previously connected with the place. He owed his preferment to William Smith, Bishop of Lincoln [1], who ruled from 1496 to 1514, and was also known to Bishops Wolsey (1514) and Atwater (1514–21). At one time I was of opinion that Ashwell had been engaged temporarily at Lincoln in 1505, but his name does not appear in the detailed list of Cathedral officials at the installation of Dean Symeon on August 14, 1506. Consequently the date of his appointment at Lincoln was not earlier than 1508.

From 1508 to 1518 Ashwell held office at Lincoln, and in the latter year was replaced by John Gilbert, who had graduated Bachelor of Music at Oxford in 1510, and who was appointed permanent organist of Lincoln Cathedral in 1524.

---

[1] Bishop Smith founded some exhibitions for choristers in the Lincoln Song School.

Thomas Ashwell

'GOD SAVE KING HERRY'. THOS. ASHWELL.
(Reconstructed from Cambridge MSS.)

57

Early Tudor Composers

In regard to the English Anthem written for the nuptials of Henry VII and Elizabeth of York in 1486, Miss Agnes Strickland, in her *Lives of the Queens of England*, makes the following statement :

> An Anthem was written for the occasion in which a strong resemblance will be immediately traced to ' God Save the King ' ; the similarity of the music is still stronger.

It is added :

> This Anthem was found with other ancient papers in the church-chest at Gayton, Northamptonshire [1]. The date is 1486. It is set to music of the old square form, and with the baritone clef on the third line :

> God save King Herry wheresoe'er he be,
>> And for Queen Elizabeth now pray we,
>> And for all her noble progeny.
> God save the Church of Christ from any folly,
>> And for Queen Elizabeth now pray we.

We are safe in dating Ashwell's creative period as between the years 1485–1515, and he disappears after the year 1517 ; for, as has been seen, his successor (John Gilbert) was appointed in 1518.

To the student who would make himself acquainted with Ashwell's works, a visit to several libraries is necessary, as his manuscripts are scattered. Some are in the British Museum, others are in the Bodleian, while a few are to be met with in Cambridge University Library.

In the British Museum (Harleian MS. 1709) there is the setting of the ' Stabat Mater ' previously alluded to, also a beautiful Motet, ' Te matrem Dei laudamus ' ; but Mr. H. B. Collins (to whom I am indebted for much information on Ashwell's compositions) kindly informs me that this Motet is correctly attributed to Hugh Aston, in proof of which he quotes Bodleian

---

[1] The Rector of Gayton kindly informs me in a letter dated December 20, 1920, that there are no documents prior to 1558 at Gayton. Miss Strickland was evidently misinformed.

Thomas Ashwell

c. 1–5, Cambridge University, and St. John's. This Harleian MS. 1709 is a Medius Part only. The British Museum (Add. MS. 30520) also has a fragment (two leaves) of his 'Mass of St. Cuthbert', and a Motet (bass only) 'Sancta Maria' (Add. MS. 34191).

The Bodleian Music School Library (e. 376–382) has two Masses by Ashwell, namely, Mass 'Ave Maria' and Mass 'Jesu Christe' —both complete.

At Cambridge University Library (MS. 815) is his remarkable five-part Mass, 'God save King Herry'—but c.т. only, not tenor, as in the Catalogue—of which the bass part is in the Library of St. John's College, Cambridge (No. 234).[1]

In conclusion, it may be well to note that the inclusion of Ashwell's song, 'She may be called a soverant lady' in Wynkyn de Worde's printed Song Book, dated October 10, 1530, is no certain proof that he was then alive. This unique music-book of twenty songs, contains compositions by Cornish, who died in 1523, and by Dr. Fayrfax, whose death occurred in 1521 ; consequently the appearance of a song by Ashwell in 1530 cannot be quoted as evidence, and we are forced to the inevitable belief that his death occurred soon after the year 1518. At the same time, it is remarkable that a certain Thomas Ashwell was in receipt of an annuity from King Henry VIII in September 1543. And it is significant that his name appears in the same list of pensioners as William Crane, Master of the Children of the Chapel Royal, Richard Bowyer, Henry Stephenson, and Thomas Byrd.

[1] Mr. H. B. Collins obligingly sent me a transcript of his own reconstruction of the opening bars of the Gloria, giving the theme of ' God save King Herry ', but I may add that it bears no resemblance to the National Anthem.

XV. *Richard Davy*

ONE of the most attractive items in the programme of the Holy Week music at Westminster Cathedral in 1921 was the performance of the four-part Passion for Palm Sunday, by Richard Davy, probably the earliest example of Passion Music by an English composer. Sir Richard Terry describes it as ' smooth, easy, and flowing; it displays a very high standard of contrapuntal technique; but, above all, it is expressive, virile, and dramatic '. This most interesting composition is found in an early sixteenth-century manuscript belonging to Eton College; though, alas! through vandalism, only forty-three perfect compositions remain out of the ninety-eight which appear in the Index. Of these forty-three, Richard Davy contributed six, namely, ' O Domine celi terreque creator ' (five parts), ' In honore summe matris ' (five parts), ' Salve Jesu Mater vere ' (five parts), ' Virgo Templum ' (five voices), ' Gaude flore virginali ' (six voices, incomplete), and ' Salve Regina ' (five parts). The ' Pryke-Song ' books belonging to King's College, Cambridge, in 1529, contain an ' Autem ' by Davy, and there are other compositions by him in the Harleian MS. 1709, St. John's College, and the Cambridge University Library, as well as three three-part songs with English words in the famous Fayrfax MS. in the British Museum (Add. MSS. 5465). Two of his English carols are very interesting, namely, ' Ah! blessed Jhesu! ' and ' Ah, my hart, remember '.

Yet, though we have such admirable specimens of Davy's sacred and secular works, Sir R. Terry says that ' as a composer he is entirely unknown to-day ', and that regarding his biography very little is known save that ' he flourished in the late fifteenth and early sixteenth centuries '. Up to the present, the only details of Davy's life are in the very brief sketch of him contributed to the second edition of Grove's *Dictionary of Music and Musicians* (1904)— and these details are one solitary paragraph of less than four lines —by Mr. J. F. R. Stainer. It is as well to give the text in order

Richard Davy

to show how meagre is the information that has been hitherto unearthed regarding such a distinguished composer : ' Richard Davy or Davys, a composer of some repute, was choirman, organist, and *informator choristarum* at Magdalen College, Oxford, from 1490 to 1492.'

After patient research I have not been able thoroughly to unravel the mystery that seems to enshroud the life story of Richard Davy, yet I have succeeded in piecing together a few new facts that may serve as a basis for a future musical historian. First of all, as he was about sixteen when he entered Magdalen College, Oxford, we are safe in dating his birth about the year 1467, and, as has been seen, he was appointed Organist and Master of the Choristers of his college in 1490—remaining in office for two years. Possibly he remained at Oxford for some time longer, probably for the sake of his divinity studies, and became a priest in 1497, at which date Richard Parker was appointed organist.

The fact of Davy's being a priest in 1497 disposes of the suggestion made to me a few years ago by a clerk in the Public Record Office, that possibly he was to be identified with Richard Davy who was granted an annuity of 6d. a day on February 15, 1501. This suggestion cannot stand, because the latter namesake was ' a yeoman of the crown, and King's servant ', as is evident from the printed *Calendar of Patent Rolls of Henry VII* (1494–1509).

Richard Davy was chaplain to Sir William Boleyn in 1501, in which year was born Anne Boleyn (grand-daughter of Sir William), destined to be the unfortunate wife of Henry VIII. His name appears in deeds of the years 1505 and 1506; and in the latter year, on May 15, he was a party to a licence of alienation of the Manor of Stiffkey, in Norfolk, to the use of Sir Thomas Boleyn (Sir W. Boleyn died 1505). Another deed mentions him as one of the feoffees in a grant of the Manors of Filby, Possewyk, West Lexham, and Carbrooke (May 15, 1506), to the use of Thomas Boleyn, son and heir of William Boleyn, Knight, deceased.[1] Apparently the priest-composer was continued in the service of

---

[1] *Calendar of Patent Rolls*, 1494–1509, p. 484.

Sir Thomas Boleyn from 1506 to 1516, the principal family residence being Blickling, in Norfolk.

In regard to Sir Thomas Boleyn, whose father had married one of the co-heiresses of the Earl of Ormonde, an Irish tradition has it that Anne Boleyn was born at the Castle of Carrick-on-Suir, in 1501, or early in 1502. Certainly, the popular idea that this lady's birth took place in 1507 cannot be sustained, as she was a Dame-in-Waiting to the French Queen, Claude, in 1519— a position that could scarcely be held by a girl of twelve! Thomas, seventh Earl of Ormonde, died on August 8, 1515, leaving his immense English estates, containing seventy-two manors, to his two daughters, the elder of whom (Anne) was Dame St. Leger and the younger (Margaret) Lady Boleyn. On the following December 12, the Lord Deputy of Ireland wrote to Henry VIII in regard to Sir Thomas Boleyn's claim to a portion of the Irish estates, which was contested by Sir Piers Butler, who claimed to be eighth Earl of Ormonde. After much litigation, on October 6, 1520, a proposal of marriage was made between Sir Piers Butler and Mary Boleyn, Anne's elder sister, and an Irish Act of Parliament was passed declaring Sir Piers as lawful heir to Sir James, sixth Earl. Subsequently, Sir Thomas Boleyn was created Viscount Rochford and Earl of Wiltshire, Ormonde, and Carrick ; and Sir Piers Butler was created Earl of Ossory [1]. Henry VIII, in order to settle the family feud, as Professor Pollard writes, ' arranged for a marriage between Anne Boleyn and Sir Piers Butler ', in 1522 ; and further, in order to propitiate the Ormonde family the King appointed Sir Piers as Lord Deputy of Ireland, on March 6, 1522. Had Butler's marriage to Anne Boleyn been celebrated in 1522, how different might have been the history of England !

Meantime, Richard Davy was chaplain to Sir Thomas Boleyn from 1506 to 1516, and, as nothing further can be gleaned of him, it is natural to suppose that he died in the latter year. (Sir Thomas

---

[1] Sir Piers was forced to surrender the title of Earl of Ormonde to Sir Thomas Boleyn, Viscount Rochford, in 1527. This title Boleyn retained till his death in 1537.

Richard Davy

Boleyn died in 1538, and there is a fine brass to his memory at Hever, in Kent.) Certainly all his creative musical work that has come down ranges between the dates 1490 and 1515, and the real surprise is that his compositions are anything but ' crude '. Considering his period, his work, as Sir R. Terry writes, ' is in every way individual and original '. One feature of the Passion Music is worthy of note, for while the generality of composers give a musical setting of the *Turba*, or ' speeches and cries of the mob ', Davy, in addition, writes choral music exclusively for the dialogue between Pilate and his wife. In other words, the convention of the thirteenth to the sixteenth century was to have the Passion Music sung among three ecclesiastics, one being the first Deacon (a bass), singing the part of Christ, the second, or *Chronista* or *Evangelista* (a tenor), the narrative of the Evangelist, and the third, or *Synagoga* or *Turba* (an alto), the exclamations of the Apostles, the crowd, and others. In Davy's score, a magnificent effect is produced by the glorious setting of the words : ' Vere filius Dei erat iste ' (' Truly this was the Son of God '), assigned to the Centurion and the watchers at the Crucifixion. In opposition to the conventional method adopted by other composers, who treat these words ' in awe-stricken accents ', Davy ' makes it ring out as a triumphant confession of faith '. Although the first three *Turba* choruses are missing in the Eton MS., and though the treble and tenor parts are also missing from the four choruses which follow, Sir R. Terry has with rare skill supplied the missing choruses of the former from other portions of Davy's own music, which fit the words to perfection, and he has written new treble and tenor parts for choruses 2 to 5 in the same contrapuntal style of the composer and the period—quite a triumph of restoration.

XVI. Robert Cowper, Mus.D.

The name of Robert Cowper (also written Couper, Coper, and Cooper) is well known as a composer of the first decade of the sixteenth century; but beyond the fact of his having graduated Doctor of Music at Cambridge in 1507, very little else has hitherto been available as to his biography. The British Museum possesses several of his Masses and Motets, as well as two Madrigals for three voices, ' I have been a foster ' and ' Farewell, my joy '; while Wynkyn de Worde's printed Song Book of 1530 has three items by him, namely, ' In youth, in age ', ' So great unkindness ', and ' Ut, re, mi ', each for three voices. A song of his, ' Petyously constrayned am I ', is in the Brit. Mus. Royal MSS., App. 58, and a Round or Catch, ' Alone I live ', was published by the Plain-Song and Medieval Music Society in 1891.

Robert Cowper was born about the year 1474, and on November 16, 1498, was presented by the Crown to " the free Chapel of Snodhill (co. Hereford), in the diocese of Hereford, vacant by the surrender of Robert Fayrefax, one of the Gentlemen of the King's Chapel, resigned ", as is recorded on the Patent Rolls. From this it would appear that Cowper, if not attached to the Court of Henry VII, was *persona grata* in courtly circles.[1]

In 1507 Robert Cowper graduated Mus.D. at Cambridge University. The entry on the Cambridge Register reads as follows [2]: ' 1507. Item, conceditur magistro Roberto Cowper ut studium quinque annorum cum practica totidem annorum citra introitum suum in eadem sufficiat sini ad incipiendum in Musice ' (Cambridge Grace Book, Gammar, p. 3a).

Previous writers have absolutely no details of Cowper after the year 1502, but it is certain that he retained the Chaplaincy of Snodhill from 1498 to 1514. This we know from the Patent

[1] According to Venn's *Alumni Cantabrigienses* (1922) Cowper graduated Mus. Bac. in 1493, and was Rector of Faulkborne (Essex) 1494–1502.

[2] This is quoted by Mr. C. F. Abdy Williams in his admirable little book on *Musical Degrees*.

Robert Cowper, Mus.D.

Rolls, inasmuch as on November 4, 1514, Robert Geffrey was presented to the free chapel of Snodhill in the room of 'Robert Cowper, clk, doctor of music, resigned ' (*Calendar of Patent Rolls*).

In 1515 Dr. Cowper's elder brother, William Cowper, was presented to the Deanery of Bridgenorth. An entry under date of January 1516 reveals this clerical Doctor of Music as the composer of ' an anthem of defuse musicke '. Three months later, on April 21, he was appointed Rector of East Horsley, in Surrey, in the Deanery of Croydon. A few weeks afterwards, on May 13, he resigned this preferment in favour of a more lucrative one, namely, the rectory of Latchington, Essex, with an annexed chapelry.

His madrigal of ' I have been a foster ' was probably sung in the play presented by Cornish at Windsor on June 15, 1522, in which a keeper, three foresters, and four hunters took part, as well as six Children of the Chapel Royal.

On June 5, 1525, William Cowper, Dean of Bridgenorth, wrote to Cromwell recommending his brother Robert for further preferment. In the letter, which is calendared in the *Calendar of Letters and Papers of Henry VIII*, the Dean urges Cromwell to procure another benefice for ' his brother Sir Robert who is well disposed and virtuous, and a good *quereman* '.

In the Inventory of the ' Pryke Song ' books belonging to King's College, Cambridge, in 1529, we find an entry of ' 4 smaller books covered with leather having Cornysh's and Coper's Masses ', evidently indicating that Cowper had composed Masses.

It would appear that Dr. Cowper was a friend of Nicholas Ludford, the composer, whose memoir appears on p. 72 of the present volume. As for the further career of Cowper himself, I can find no trace after the year 1529, and I presume he died about that time, when he would have been a sexagenarian. His creative period was between the years 1495 and 1526, and his best work is regarded as quite equal to that of John Taverner or of Redford. He must not be confounded with a later namesake, John Cooper or Cowper, who Italianized his name as Coperario in 1598, and who died in 1627.

XVII. *John Lloyd*

In the closing years of the fifteenth century Welsh musicians began to give evidence of their Celtic inheritance, and at this date several of them were either in the service of the Chapel Royal or were attached to the Court as minstrels. Our next chapter will treat of the career of Robert Jones, and now there is the question of John Lloyd, a famous priest-composer ; yet, save for the very brief notice of him by Sir John Hawkins, no biographical data can be gleaned in our usual books of reference. His name has been written ' Floyd ' and ' Flude '—a not unusual form of the Welsh surname Lloyd—and although Hawkins places him under Henry VIII, he had previously belonged to the Chapel of King Henry VII, as will be seen.

The first notice of John Lloyd is in the year 1504–5, when he appears as one of the priests of the Chapel Royal, from which circumstance it is fair to conclude that he was born *circa* 1480. Evidently he soon got into favour, inasmuch as there is an entry in the Patent Rolls dated September 18, 1506, recording his appointment to the parish church of Munslow, diocese of Hereford, void by resignation (*Calendar of Patent Rolls of Henry VII*, vol. ii, p. 499).

Probably this appointment to Munslow resulted in Lloyd's leaving the Court for the diocese of Hereford in 1506 ; and this is the more likely inasmuch as his name does not appear in the official list of the King's Chapel at the funeral of Henry VII on May 11, 1509. Nor yet does he seem to have been recalled to the Chapel Royal on the accession of Henry VIII, for in the *Calendar of Letters and Papers of Henry VIII*, vol. i, second edition (1920), we do not find his name in the detailed list of the King's Chapel at the coronation on Sunday, June 24, 1509. However, about a year later he was appointed a Gentleman of the Chapel Royal, and his name appears as such among those who received liveries for the funeral of Prince Henry on February 27, 1511.

66

John Lloyd

Some of his fellow singers on that sad occasion were Dr. Fayrfax, William Crane, William Cornish, Thomas Farthing, and David Burton, whose memoirs will be found among the present series.

On November 12, 1511, there was a warrant issued to give John Lloyd, Gentleman of the Chapel Royal, a black chamlet gown (*Calendar of Letters of Henry VIII*, vol. i, p. 478). It may be observed that William Crane, a month later, was given ' a tawny chamlet gown ' from the Great Wardrobe. (Probably black chamlet was given to the priest-singers.) Another warrant issued from the Great Wardrobe on April 16, 1512, is proof that John Lloyd (whose surname stands in the Exchequer Roll as ' Floyd ') was given ' a black velvet fur coat ', as were also Robert Penn and Thomas Farthing—both of the latter being Gentlemen of the Chapel Royal. These three also received ' gowns ' on November 3.

Previous to this, on March 20, 1512, John Lloyd had been granted a ' corrody ' in the monastery of St. Augustine's, Bristol, *vice* Edward Jones, deceased. A year later he joined the members of the Chapel Royal in attendance on King Henry VIII on his expedition to Thérouanne and Tournai, returning to London at the end of October 1513.

On October 3, 1518, John Lloyd took part in the Grand Mumming which was held at Cardinal Wolsey's Palace at Durham House in the Strand. Two years later, in June 1520, he was one of the Chapel Royal Choir at the historic Field of the Cloth of Gold —a pageant that has been frequently described. About this time he resumed a grant of ' corrody ' in the monastery of Thetford.

Meantime several deaths had thinned the ranks of the Chapel Royal, and on December 12, 1520, Thomas Farthing passed away. The last pageants in which Lloyd took part were those held on June 4 and 5 at Greenwich, in honour of the Emperor Charles V. After these he made a pilgrimage to Jerusalem in fulfilment of a vow, and having visited the Holy Places, returned to England. On his arrival he found that William Cornish had retired from the Mastership of the Children of the Chapel Royal after twenty years' service, and had been replaced by William Crane, whose

E 2

appointment was dated March 25, 1523. On the following day
Dr. John Clarke, Dean of the Chapel Royal, was promoted to
the Bishopric of Bath and Wells, being succeeded as Dean by
Dr. Richard Sampson.

John Lloyd died on April 3, 1523, and his obituary is thus
chronicled by Sir John Hawkins :

> John Floyd, of Welsh extraction, Bachelor of Music, and
> a Gentleman of the Chapel Royal, *temp*. Henry VIII. He
> made a pilgrimage to Jerusalem, returned, and died in the
> King's Chapel, and was buried in the Savoy Church, with
> the inscription : ' Johannes Floyd, virtutis et religionis cultor.
> Obiit 3 April, 1523.'

Although Hawkins styles him ' Bachelor of Music ', I have
failed to discover his name in the Oxford or Cambridge Registers.
However, the statement may be correct, as we find Ambrose
Payne, Parson of Lambeth, who died in 1528, described on his
monument—formerly to be seen in the old church of St. Dunstan's-
in-the-East—as ' a Bachelour of Musick '.

Certain it is that John Lloyd was a very capable musician and
composer. He is said to have written much sacred music, including Masses and Motets, but no doubt most of his manuscripts
disappeared after the death of Queen Mary. Fortunately, however, in Add. MSS. 31922 of the British Museum—a fine vellum
manuscript of the reign of Henry VIII—there are two pieces by
him. This valuable manuscript is of added interest inasmuch as
the composer is described as having graduated in music : ' in
armonia graduat ', which plainly points to the fact of his having
been a Bachelor of Music. No doubt it was examined by Sir John
Hawkins, and hence his statement as recorded above. At ff. 25*b*
and 31*b* will be found these two pieces, set for three voices or
instruments, the name of the composer being given as ' John
Flude ' or Floyd (Lloyd). The manuscript also contains compositions by Thomas Farthing, King Henry VIII, Robert Fayrfax,
John Dunstable, Richard Pygot, Dr. Cowper, and William
Cornish.

XVIII. *Robert Jones*

I⊤ is well perhaps to warn the reader that Robert Jones, the early Tudor composer, is quite a different person from the Robert Jones of the 'Triumphs of Oriana', for, although musicians have been credited with longevity, there is more than half a century separating the musical activities of the two composers. As a matter of fact, the earlier of the two namesakes was a Gentleman of the Chapel Royal in 1512, while the later Robert Jones was not born till about the year 1570. The early Tudor composer has the distinction of figuring among the contributors to Wynkyn de Worde's unique printed book of *Twenty Songs, IX of IIII parts and XI of III parts*, dated from London, on October 10, 1530. He is also included in Morley's oft-quoted list—published in 1597—of famous English composers who flourished before the Reformation, and hence he deserves inclusion in the present series, all the more by reason of the fact that his biography does not appear in any of our standard books of reference.

Robert Jones was born *circa* 1485, and was a boy chorister in the Chapel Royal under William Newark. On the death of Edward Johns, or Jones (who may, possibly, have been a relative), he was appointed a 'Gentleman of the King's Chapel', in March 1512, under William Cornish[1]. He accompanied King Henry VIII in the summer of 1513 as one of the Chapel Royal, and there are contemporary notices of the magnificent singing of the English monarch's chapel at Thérouanne, on September 3 following, when 'a Te Deum was sung by the King's singers', followed by 'an Anthem of Our Lady and another of St. George'. On September 17, at Tournai, in a pavilion of purple and gold, after a sermon by the Bishop of St. Asaph, a 'Te Deum' was again sung by the choristers of the Chapel Royal, led by Dr. Robert Fayrfax, under

[1] For an account of Cornish see Chapter III.

69

the direction of William Cornish, Master of the Boys. It is interesting to add that there is a German account of the Picardy campaign in the *Calendar of Letters of Henry VIII*, with an English translation, from which we learn that for amusement, ' for field music the English had a shalm player and a bagpiper who play together ', while the military music consisted of 'flutes, trumpets, and drums '.

Between the years 1514 and 1519 Jones was living at East Greenwich, as we learn from an interesting document in the *Patent Rolls of Henry VIII*. In this grant, which was formally enrolled on November 21, 1520, Thomas Farthing, Gentleman of the Chapel Royal, 'and his heirs for ever ', was constituted the owner of 'a tenement in East Greenwich, formerly in the tenure of Robert Jones '. The only rent payable for Jones's tenement was ' the service of a red rose, if it be asked '.

At the historic Field of the Cloth of Gold, in June 1520, Robert Jones was one of the Gentlemen of the Chapel Royal whose magnificent singing was much admired by French critics. On his return to England he obtained another tenement, but the new owner of his former residence, Thomas Farthing [1], did not long enjoy it, as his death occurred on December 12 of the same year (1520).

The next glimpse we get of Robert Jones is in the official ' List of the Ministers of the King's Chapel ', in the Eltham Ordinances of 1526, where his name figures as seventh in the roll of Gentlemen of the King's Chapel. Very little else seems to be chronicled of him save that he contributed to Wynkyn de Worde's Song Book of 1530, as previously stated. In this unique collection, now housed in the British Museum, Jones is represented by a song, ' Who shall have my fair lady ', set for three voices.

I can find no trace of Robert Jones after the year 1535, so it is safe to conclude that he died about that date. The appearance, however, of the name R. Jones in a document of the year 1538 at one time led me to imagine that, probably, this reference was

---

[1] For an account of Thomas Farthing see **Chapter XIII**.

to the early Tudor composer, but an examination of the original record revealed the fact that the person therein named was in reality a certain Richard Jones, who turned out to be 'Chief Master of St. Paul's School'—quite a different personage. In any case, the position of Robert Jones as Gentleman of the Chapel Royal was filled up in 1536, certainly before the year 1537.

As regards his compositions, we have previously alluded to his song in Wynkyn de Worde's book (1530), and to his fame as a composer, on the testimony of Morley. However, there is more tangible evidence of his powers in his Mass and Magnificat, both of which are among the Peterhouse MSS. The former, the Mass 'Spes Nostra', will be found in manuscripts both at Peterhouse, Cambridge, and in Add. MS. 34191. It may be noted that the tenor part is wanting. Further, the name of the composer appears in the manuscript as 'Robard Joonys'. The latter manuscript displays much invention, even from a cursory examination, and, together with the Mass, ought to be printed by the Carnegie Trust or the British Music Society. It is a distinct advance on the technique of Cornish and Crane, and shows a glimmering of the great polyphonic work afterwards achieved by Tallis and Byrd, though, it must be added, it is not to be compared with Ludford.

XIX. *Nicholas Ludford*

GREAT as is the reputation of Robert Fayrfax, there is another
early Tudor composer whose works may bear favourable comparison with his : this man is Nicholas Ludford. And yet it is
only since the beginning of the present century that Ludford may
be said to have been ' discovered '. His compositions are almost
as numerous as those of Fayrfax, and hence we are in a position
to estimate their value. Even Sir R. Terry recently admitted
that Ludford's works ' show him to be a much bigger man ' than
he had at first suspected ; and—stronger proof still—the general
verdict of musical critics who have been given an opportunity
of hearing seven of Ludford's Masses sung during the past few
years at Westminster Cathedral, has confirmed the expert views
of H. B. Collins, Davey, Terry, and Walker. I was hoping that
Mr. Orsmond Anderton, in his recent book on *Early English
Music* (1920), would throw some new light on the biography of
this important composer, but, alas ! he writes thus :

> No information as to his life is available except that he
> was about contemporaneous with, possibly a little later than,
> Fayrfax. Several of his Masses are in use at Westminster
> Cathedral, including seven for three voices, one for each
> day in the week. Of these perhaps the finest is the ' Missa
> Sabbato '.

Mr. H. B. Collins writes in an almost similar strain in his
excellent paper on ' Latin Church Music by Early English Composers ', Part 2, in the *Proceedings of the Musical Association*
(1916–17) :

> Another composer of about the same period as Fayrfax, or
> slightly later, was Nicholas Ludford, with regard to whom
> I have been able to ascertain no particulars whatever. His
> name does not appear in Grove, nor in the *Dictionary of*

Nicholas Ludford

National Biography, though he is mentioned at the end of Morley's *Plaine and Easie Introduction* as one of the composers whose works the author had consulted.

Thus it may be briefly stated that hitherto the biographical data regarding Ludford was *nil*, save that he was more or less the contemporary of Fayrfax ; that is to say, we may assume him to have flourished in the years 1495–1521. A diligent search has revealed a few more facts regarding this early Tudor composer. It may be well to note, however, that he was not, as generally surmised, a member of the Chapel Royal. Doubtless a further investigation may bring to light more details, but meantime the following notices may be helpful, though the net result has not been as fruitful as could be desired.

Nicholas Ludford first appears in an account book of the Steward of Ashby Leger, in March 1520, printed in the *Calendar of Letters and Papers of Henry VIII* (vol. iii). At one time I was inclined to believe that Ludford was a member of the Chapel Royal, and a friend told me that his name occurred in some accounts in the Public Record Office, in connexion with the Dean of the King's Chapel, Dr. John Clark. An examination of the Calendar, however, revealed the fact that although the accounts of the Dean of the Chapel are given for March 1520, Ludford's name does not appear in them; yet his name does occur in the succeeding entry recording the payment of £119 8s. by a number of persons in the Steward's Account of Ashby Leger (Northampton). Moreover, in the detailed account of the Chapel Royal at the Field of the Cloth of Gold, in 1520, Ludford's name is not to be found. In 1520 he seems to have been a contemporary of John Kite, who had been sub-dean of the Chapel Royal, and was promoted to be Archbishop of Armagh. Consequently, he would then be about forty years of age, from which we may safely place his birth as *circa* 1480.

The next notice of Nicholas Ludford, who was married in 1535, is on July 3, 1538, when he was granted an exemption ' from serving on juries and from being made escheator, coroner, collector of taxes, constable, or other officer '. This notice is to be found in the *Calendar of Letters, &c., of Henry VIII*, and it may be assumed that the exemption arose from Ludford's connexion with the Court, and was probably due to some serious accident or illness, for it could scarcely be on the score of old age, as the composer was then on the sunny side of sixty.

Evidently Ludford died in 1541, or early in 1542, as on June 1, 1542, among the Life Grants in the King's Books (33 Henry VIII), there is an entry of a lease for twenty-one years to Elizabeth Ludford, widow, of certain lands and a water-mill in Birmingham Manor, Warwickshire. Through the courtesy of Mr. H. B. Collins, I am enabled to give the following list of Ludford's works, all as yet in manuscript :

> Six Masses for solo and three-part chorus, each containing a Sequence (Brit. Mus., R. Appen. 45–47).
> Missa ' Benedicta ', for six voices (Lambeth and Caius).   In the former manuscript it is given anonymously.
> Missa ' Videte Miraculum ', for six voices (manuscript at Caius, Cambridge).
> Missa ' Christi Virgo ', for five voices (manuscripts at Caius and Peterhouse).
> Missa ' Inclina Domine ', for five voices (Peterhouse).
> Missa ' Lapidaverunt Stephanum ', for five voices (Lambeth —but anonymously—and Caius).
> Missa ' Regnum mundi ', for five voices (Peterhouse).
> Missa ' Le Roy '—only fragmentary (Brit. Mus. Add. 30520).
> Magnificat, for six voices (Caius).
> Ave Marie Ancilla, for five voices (Peterhouse).
> Ave Cujus Conceptio, for five voices (Peterhouse).
> Domine Jesu Christi, for five voices (Peterhouse).
> Salve Regina (No. 1), medius only (Harley, 1709).
> Salve Regina (No. 2) (Harley and Peterhouse).   (N.B.—The Peterhouse MS. wants the tenor.)

Mr. Collins has scored many of these Masses—written in ' black void ' notation—and he gives the following estimate of the first of the six Masses for solo bass voice or unison chorus, alternating with a three-part choir. It is also worthy of note that the Canto Fermo, in plainchant, is in ' strictly measured music ' like that of the chorus :

The counterpoint is at least as fluent and facile as that of Fayrfax, and is also of a rather more advanced character, the parts often entering one after another with points of imitation, showing a transition to a later style. The whole composition is lighter in character than Fayrfax's work, partly owing to the use of only three voices, and also owing to the fact that in most of the movements the greater prolation is substituted for perfect time, though the latter is used for the Sanctus and Agnus. The Mass is founded on the same melody as that used by Taverner in his Kyrie entitled ' Ley Roy '. The Credo is set complete without any omissions, and the Mass also includes a setting of a lengthy Sequence, ' Ave praeclara Maris stella ', which occurs in the Sarum Gradual on the Octave of the Assumption. The Mass is altogether an interesting composition, which makes one desire to know more of the author's work.

XX. *Sir William Hawte*

CONSIDERABLE confusion has been caused by the very name of this composer, for the simple reason that the prefix ' Sir ' was applied to a priest as well as to a knight, but inasmuch as some of the manuscripts containing compositions by Hawte definitely gave his full name as ' Sir William Hawte, *miles* ', there is no question but that the composer is to be equated with a knight and not with a priest.   However, strange as it may seem, there has been a new difficulty over the identity of the particular *miles*, for it appears that there were two individuals of the same name almost contemporaneous ; at least, there were two knights of that name who flourished one under Henry VII and the other under Henry VIII.   Yet the difficulty is easily solved, inasmuch as experts are agreed that the manuscripts containing Hawte's compositions are almost certainly prior to the year 1500 ; in fact, the Pepysian Catalogue, MS. 1236, is tentatively dated as from the period of King Edward IV, that is to say, from 1461–82.   Neither Burney nor Hawkins furnishes any biographical data for this early Tudor composer, and Mr. Henry Davey gives no help save that he prefers to date the period of Hawte's activity as ' 1480–1500 ' (*History of English Music*, new edition, 1921, p. 81).   As will be seen, Hawte flourished under Henry VI, Edward IV, Richard III, and Henry VII.

Sir William Hawte was son of William Hawte, Esquire, who made his will on May 9, 1462, and who desired that his body was to be buried with his two wives in the church of the Austin Friars, Canterbury, before the statue of St. Catherine.   The first mention in official records of William Hawte is on May 19, 1457, when he received a commission to see about the erection of beacons on the sea-coast.   In this commission he is styled ' William Hawte the younger '—his father being still alive ; and we may therefore assume that he was then over twenty-one years of age, which

76

Sir William Hawte

would place his birth as *circa* 1436. His father died in 1464, and on November 23, 1465, the name of ' William Hawte, Knight ', appears in a commission regarding forfeitures. In 1468 (October 9) he was one of the commissioners for musters at Sandwich ; and in the following year was a commissioner of array (October 29, 1469)—said commission being renewed in the years 1470 and 1471.

Between the years 1471 and 1474 Sir William Hawte was an important county magnate, and in 1475 he appears as Sheriff of Kent. So highly was he esteemed by Edward IV that the King, on May 29, 1478, granted him for life an annuity of twenty marks from the previous Michaelmas (*Cal. Pat. Rolls*, p. 100). In 1481 Sir William Hawte, senior, and William Hawte, junior, were joined in a commission.

Under Richard III we find other important commissions given to Sir William Hawte between the years 1483 and 1485 ; and he was in equal favour with Henry VII, who, on December 9, 1485, appointed him, with others, ' to deliver the gaol of the castle of Canterbury for this turn '—a similar commission being given him on October 16, 1487 (*Cal. Pat. Rolls, Henry VII*, pp. 70 and 213). On May 26, 1490, he was appointed a commissioner of array, and on April 5, 1491, he received another commission. His name appears first on the list of commissioners appointed to deliver the gaol of the castle of Canterbury on March 7, 1492, and again on October 28, 1493.

Meantime, between the years 1475 and 1495 Sir William Hawte had devoted much time to his musical studies, and co-operated with the great Benedictine Prior Selling in furthering learning in the Claustral School of Canterbury. From internal evidence there is good reason to believe that Hawte's musical compositions date from this period, that is, during the last quarter of the fifteenth century—practically coincident with the rule of William Selling, who was Prior of Christ Church, Canterbury, from 1472 to 1495. Selling, like Hawte, was also in favour with Henry VII, who appointed him one of his ambassadors to the Pope in 1486. And it is of interest to note that, as will be seen in Chapter XXVIII,

77

John Dygon studied at the monastic school of Canterbury, where he was a novice between the years 1497 and 1504.

On July 13, 1495, Hawte was joined in a commission for County Kent, figuring with such notabilities as the Duke of Buckingham, the Marquis of Dorset, the Earl of Arundel, the Earl of Oxford, the Earl of Northumberland, the Earl of Shrewsbury, and others. He received a similar commission on June 20, 1496, and again on October 24 of same year.

A close search of the Patent Rolls does not reveal any later mention of Hawte, and it is fair to assume that he died in 1498 or 1499, certainly before 1500. It is well to note that his name was variously spelled ' Haut ', ' Haute ', and ' Hawte ' ; and it is well known that the Hauts were important county people of Kent in the twelfth to fifteenth centuries. As Canon Jenkins writes in his *Diocesan History of Canterbury*, apropos some of the greater houses failing prior to the sixteenth century, ' the Hautes ', like the Pluckleys and Surrendens, ' failed in the male line ', and we can thus conclude that Sir William Hawte died without issue in 1498 or 1499. The property then passed to his brother, Sir Thomas Hawte, who died early in 1503, leaving a son William, whose wardship was granted to Sir Henry Frowyk and Thomas Jakes, on July 20, 1503 (*Cal. Pat. Rolls, Henry VII*, 1494–1509, p. 308), and whose name first appears in a commission of March 1512–13.

As to the value of Hawte's compositions the specimens that remain are sufficient to stamp him as a not unworthy disciple of the school of Newark and Fayrfax. He was certainly a gifted musical amateur, as is revealed in his beautiful five-part ' Benedicamus Domino ' in the Pepysian MS. 1236. Other compositions by him will be found in the same MS., and also in Add. MS. 5665 in the British Museum.

XXI. *William Pasche*

In the oft-quoted Addendum to Morley's *Plaine and Easie Introduction to Practicall Musicke*, in 1597, among the names of the Early Tudor 'Practitioners' pride of place is given to ' Mr. Pashe '. It is to be observed that in Morley's list the name of ' Mr.' or ' Master ' is given to Pasche, Byrd, Tallis, White, Parsons, Wilkinson, Sturton, and Risby, showing that these were ' Masters of Arts ', or else outstanding ' Masters of Musicke '. Thus, the reputation of Master Pasche must have been very great, even among a race of giants.

The name Pashe or Pasche—also written Passhe—occurs under Henry VI, Edward IV, and Henry VII, and we find a Master Thomas Pasche as Prebendary of Windsor from 1449 to 1474, he being also sub-almoner to King Henry VI. Possibly this Canon of Windsor was an uncle or relative of William Pasche.

Biographical data, up to the present, as to William Pasche may be described as *nil*, and the only information to be found in the new edition of Mr. Henry Davey's *History of English Music* (1921) is one solitary sentence as follows :

> William Pashe (Pasche) may have been the Pashe whose will was proved in 1525 ; but I should have supposed his period rather earlier, perhaps 1430–1500.

Let me here say at once that William Pasche was the Pashe whose will was proved in 1525 ; and his period was not so early as ' 1430–1500 ', but probably from 1460–1515. Yet though scanty details are forthcoming of Pasche's biography, we are fortunate in having ample evidence of his musical powers. Admirable specimens of his gifts are to be found at Cambridge—namely, at Caius and St. John's, at Peterhouse, and at the University Library. The musical manuscripts at St. John's and Cambridge

79

Early Tudor Composers

University may be dated as *circa* 1515, while those at Peterhouse are not so early—probably *circa* 1540.

Pasche's greatest work is his delightful Mass, ' Christus resurgens ', of which Caius College possesses the complete parts, while Cambridge University has a contra-tenor part and St. John's a bass part. A beautiful Motet of his, ' Sancta Maria ', is at Peterhouse, and it is described by Mr. Henry Davey as ' an attractive piece allied in spirit to Josquin's " Ave vera virginitas " '. There is also a Magnificat by Pasche at Peterhouse, though it would seem, from Dr. Jebb's list, that formerly there were two Magnificats in that Library. Portions of a Mass by Pasche are in the Cambridge University Library, and there is a Motet by him in the British Museum among the Add. MSS. 5665—at least if we are to assume that the piece marked as by ' W. P.' is to be identified with William Pasche. I may here observe that an ingenious friend suggested to me that ' W. P.' may have been meant for William Parsons, who harmonized eighty-one Psalms in Day's edition of 1563 ; but the British Museum MS. containing the Motet is apparently of the early years of the sixteenth century ; in fact, the dates ' 1510 ' and ' 1511 ' are to be found in it—much too early for Parsons.

In regard to the biography of Pasche very few facts have come down. The late Dr. Cummings, in answer to an inquiry of mine, gave it as his opinion that the composer was attached to the Chapel Royal or the Court. After a close search of the various lists of these two royal establishments, I could find no name resembling that of Pasche. A further search of the lists of various cathedral establishments yielded no better results, nor was I more successful in a careful examination of the Patent Rolls, nor yet in a search of Hennessy's ' Novum Repertorium '. At length, when I had almost abandoned hope, I made a search of fifteenth-century wills, and was rewarded with a clue to the family of the composer. Following up this clue, I was fortunate enough to run to earth this elusive composer, who I have good reason to believe belonged to the Chapel of the Duchess of Exeter, sister of King Edward IV, about the year 1479. I also discovered that

Missa 'Christus resurgens'.

SANCTUS.

Caius MS. 667.
Cambr. University, 815 Contratenor.

WM. PASCHE.
Reconstructed by H. B. COLLINS.

N.B.—This extract is printed by permission of the Master and Fellows of Gonville and Caius College, Cambridge, and also by permission of the Librarian of Cambridge University.

Sanc - - - - - - - - - - - - - - - -

- tus,   Sanc - - - - - - - - - - - - - -

- tus,   Sanc - - - - - - - - - -

- - - - - -   Sanc - - - - - - - - -

- tus,   Sanc - - - - - - - - - -

- tus,   Sanc - - - - - - - - -

Camb. Un.
- - tus, ...   Sanc - - - - -

- - - - tus, . .   Sanc - - - -

Sanc - - - - -

- - - - - - - - - - - - tus. . . . . .

- - - - - - - - - - - tus. . . . . .

- - - - - - - - - - - - - tus.

- - - - - - - - - - - tus.

- - - - - - - - tus. . . . . .

* Caius.
- - tus, ... Sanc - - &c.

William Pasche

a Richard Pasche—probably a younger brother or a nephew of
the composer—was one of the Wardens of the Guild of Holy
Trinity of New Windsor in 1513.

William Pasche was one of the Gentlemen of the Chapel of
Anne, Duchess of Exeter, in 1476, so we can safely assume the
date of his birth as *circa* 1450. The Duchess—who was sister to
King Edward IV and Richard III—died in 1480, having taken
for her second husband Sir Thomas St. Leger, who was granted
a licence on March 30, 1481, to found a perpetual chantry of two
chaplains in the Chapel Royal, Windsor, to be called ' the Chantry
of Anne, late Duchess of Exeter '. Of course, the attainder of
Sir Thomas St. Leger and the death of King Edward IV (April 9,
1483) must have affected the chances of promotion for Pasche
under Richard III.

It is not a little remarkable that the few facts we do know of
the biography of Pasche are derived from two wills—one proved
in 1516 and the other in 1525. In the former will, made by
Richard Gumby, chaplain to the Duchess of Exeter, a bequest
was made to the Church of Compton, in Gloucestershire, and to
Master Stratford (chaplain to King Edward IV), also to Master
Newman and *Master Pasche*. This will was proved on May 29,
1516, by John Veysey, Dean of the Chapel Royal (*Cal. Lett.
Hen. VIII*, 1515–18, part 1, p. 566).

Apparently Pasche had to live in retirement during the reigns
of King Richard III (1483–5) and of Henry VII (1485–1509),
and we hear no more of him till his death in 1525. He made his
will on May 17, 1525, and directed that his body was to be buried
' in the chancel of St. Margaret's Church in Friday Street, in
London '. He bequeathed the sum of xii*d*. to the high altar of
the same church, and a similar sum to the high altar of Dursley
(Gloucestershire) :

> The Residue of my goods not bequeathed, my funeral and
> my debts paid, I give them to Alice, my Wife, and to John,
> my son, the which I make my two executors for to dispose
> them for the health of my Soul and all Christian souls, with

the supervision of John Hyskins and Thomas Hevyn, they to have for their labours both xxvi*s*. viii*d*.

The will is witnessed by Stephen Padley, priest, Watkyn Woodward, and William Clotesboke, with others.

Pasche must have died a few weeks later, as the will was proved on July 12, 1525, in the Cathedral Church of St. Paul's, London.

XXII. *Richard Sampson*

Of the many distinguished composers who flourished during the reign of Henry VIII the name of Richard Sampson holds an honoured place. Dr. Ernest Walker, in his excellent *History of Music in England*, and Henry Davey, give prominence to Sampson, but as to biographical data none is furnished save that he was 'Dean of the Chapel Royal in 1516'—an error of date, as will be seen in the course of the present chapter. No previous musical writer has taken the trouble to piece together the scattered references to this remarkable ecclesiastic and composer to be found in the *Calendar of Letters and Papers of Henry VIII*, and I confess it was no easy task to wade through the twenty volumes (in reality thirty-one parts) of that monumental work, on which account the material unearthed will be serviceable to future investigators of early Tudor music.

To begin with, Richard Sampson, LL.D., was not Dean of the Chapel Royal in 1516. This coveted position, which was generally the prelude to a bishopric, was held by John Vesey during 1514–19 (in which latter year he was made Bishop of Exeter), and by John Clark during 1519–23.

In 1511 Sampson received payment of £10 from Sir Robert Southwell on a diplomatic errand to Antwerp. In 1513–16 he was in the service of Wolsey, and was his representative at Tournai; Archdeacon of Dorset in 1514–16, and Proctor of Tournai, January 12, 1517. Three years later he appears as Dean of St. Stephen's, Westminster, and on April 1, 1522, he was given the canonry of St. Paul's Cathedral, vacant by the death of C. Urswick, to which post was added on June 29 the sacristship of St. Paul's. At length, after the appointment of Dr. John Clark as Bishop of Bath and Wells (March 26, 1523), and his restitution of temporalities (May 2), Richard Sampson was promoted to the Deanery of the Chapel Royal at a salary of £33 6s. 8d. a year.

In the King's Book of Expenses for 1532 we meet with an item under date August 11 : ' To Master Dean of the King's Chapel [Dr. Sampson], the ordinary reward for the Chapel, 40s.' Not long afterwards, on March 13, 1533, Dr. Sampson was granted the Prebend of Stotfield in the diocese of Lichfield, and four months later (July 9) he was given the Deanery of Lichfield. He was thus a super-pluralist, enjoying the revenues of Dean of St. Stephen's, Dean of the Chapel Royal, and Dean of Lichfield, as well as Dean of Windsor. Further preferment awaited him, because on March 31, 1534, he was presented to the rectory of Hackney, but as a sort of set-off he resigned the vicarage of Stepney.

Owing to the illness of Dean Pace of St. Paul's, it was found necessary to have a Vice-Dean, and hence on February 20, 1536, Cromwell appointed Sampson ' Coadjutor '. Consequently, on Pace's death in June 1536, we are not surprised to find Sampson promoted to the Deanery of St. Paul's, followed by his promotion to the see of Chichester on June 11, obtaining restitution of the temporalities on July 4. He was subsequently (July 20) dispensed to hold the Deanery of St. Paul's (of which Whytbroke was sub-Dean) *in commendam*, having previously resigned the Deanery of Windsor.

Yet although Bishop Sampson owed so much to royal favour, he was a stout partisan of the old faith. On August 21, 1538, he wrote to a dignitary at Rye expressing his aversion to any service sung openly in English, and advising the non-adoption of ' such novelties '. He was imprisoned in the Tower on May 29, 1540, for sending an alms to Blessed Thomas Abell. As Dr. Gairdner writes : ' Sampson, Bishop of Chichester, was one morning nominated as the first Bishop of Westminster ; two hours later he was disgraced and imprisoned.' However, he was soon released, but was replaced as Dean of the Chapel Royal by Thirlby, the new Bishop of Westminster. As a solatium he was promoted by Henry VIII to the see of Lichfield and Coventry on March 3,

Richard Sampson

1543, receiving the temporalities of the same on March 14. In the Royal MSS. 11 e. xi are two fine Motets by Sampson, one for four voices and the other for five voices, namely, 'Psallite felices' (in honour of King Henry VIII) and 'Quam pulchra es amica', printed in the *Oxford History of Music*, vol. ii.

It does not come within the scope of this brief memoir to touch on the career of Sampson as Bishop of Lichfield, but he was one of the six bishops that voted for retaining the old Service books. His musical career practically ended in 1540. There is much obscurity about his religious views under Edward VI, and it is most probable that inwardly he adhered to the old faith. He died at Eccleshall on September 25, 1554, almost eighty years of age, and was buried in the parish church there.

XXIII. *Simon Burton*

CONSIDERABLE confusion has been caused, owing to the fact that two composers of the name of Burton flourished almost contemporaneously, with the result that most of our musical historians have regarded them as one person and have so treated them, crediting all the musical activities of the two to one single individual, Davy Burton or Avery Burton, whose career has been set forth in my second chapter ('David Burton'). Yet it is certain that there were two musicians named Burton who flourished under Henry VIII, but while one was known as Davy or Avery, the other was called Simon. Moreover, David Burton was the earlier of the two, and reference is made to him under Henry VII in 1494, whereas Simon Burton does not come into prominence till 1516. It is not at all unlikely that David Burton was styled 'Davy' or 'Avery', in order to distinguish him from Simon Burton, especially as both were attached to the Court.

Simon Burton was attached to the household of Henry VIII in the year 1518 as yeoman of the Crown, and on October 24 was granted 6*d.* a day Crown fee, *vice* James Garside, deceased. On June 17, 1528, William Huchins, Gentleman of the Chapel Royal, was granted the corrody in the monastery of Tywardreth, Cornwall, *vice* Simon Burton, resigned ; the reason of this resignation is that soon after we find Burton in possession of a corrody in the monastery of St. Augustine's, Bristol. This corrody he surrendered in January 1533, and on February 4 it was given to William ap Howell, one of the Marshals of the King's Hall.

In 1534 he entered the service of the Princess Mary, and taught her the Virginals [1]—an instrument on which she was already fairly proficient. From a letter written by the Bishop of Tarbes,

---

[1] I suspect that Simon ' Burton ' and not ' Paston ' was the Princess's Music Master. Paston may be a scribal error.

Simon Burton

one of the French Ambassadors, in the autumn of the year 1535, we learn that the Princess 'amused herself while the Ambassadors were with Elizabeth, by playing on the Virginals'.

After the death of Queen Katherine on January 8, 1536, and the execution of Anne Boleyn in May, the Princess Mary was allowed an establishment of her own, consisting of forty-two persons, and on August 30 was proclaimed heiress apparent to the English throne. The death of Jane Seymour, on October 24, 1537, naturally improved the position of Mary, and we are given many notices of Simon Burton during 1536–45 in the Privy Purse Expenses of the Princess Mary, edited by Sir Frederick Madden in 1831.

On December 10, 1536, Simon Burton received a *douceur* of twenty shillings from the Princess—followed at Christmas by a similar amount (almost equal to £20 of our present money), and we find that his actual salary was £4 a year, paid quarterly. In March, June, and September of 1537, Burton's payments are duly recorded, and in September 1537 he received a bonus of 11s. 3d., while the regular quarterly payments of 20s. are entered for the years 1538 and 1539, with several extra 'tips'.

An interesting entry, under date July 1538, reveals the fact that Simon Burton was a married man, as we read that Princess Mary gave five shillings to Burton himself and a similar sum to 'Symon Burton's wife'. The Princess must have derived considerable benefit from Burton's teaching, because in a letter from the Ambassador Chapuys to the Queen of Hungary in 1538 he describes 'her admirable playing on the lute and virginals'.

Burton received his accustomed salary quarterly during the years 1539–43, and in November of the latter year received twenty shillings 'payment in advance'. In January 1544 he received a like sum 'for his New Year's gift', and the diplomatic musician sent a present of 'Capons and pudding' to the Princess. In October 1544 the Princess gave Charley Morley 13s. 4d. 'for Symon Burton', and 6s. 8d. to Lady Kempe for him. He was also paid the usual Christmas quarterly present of 20s. in December 1544.

Early Tudor Composers

The last reference I have met with concerning Simon Burton is on December 25, 1545, in the King's Book of Payments, from which it appears he had a quarterly salary of 50*s*. as ' player on the Virginals '. He probably died soon after, and his name does not appear in King Edward VI's establishment nor in that of Queen Mary.

XXIV. *William Whytbroke*

THE name of William Whytbroke is familiar to all students of John Day's *Certaine Notes set forthe in foure and three partes to be song at the Mornynge, Communion, and Evening Praier,* a rare work published in 1560 containing his 'Let your light so shine'. Other pieces by him include the added tenor part to Taverner's beautiful Latin motet,[1] 'Audivi media nocte' (to be found in Add. MSS., Brit. Mus., 17802–17805), endorsed, 'Pars ad placitum W. Whitbroke fecit'. In addition the well-known Mass, 'Upon the square ' (Add. MSS., Brit. Mus.), testifies to his powers as a composer. But, again, as has been so frequently stated in the present book, the biography of Whytbroke has long remained a desideratum. Mr. Royle Shore[2], in an excellent paper on 'The Early Harmonized Chants of the Church of England ', recently admitted that as regards Whytbroke and Knight, nothing apparently is known.

As will be seen, it is quite a mistake to imagine that Whytbroke composed to any extent under Elizabeth : the fact is that his creative period was during the years 1530–56, and all his best work was written on the lines of the ancient Catholic liturgy. He also indulged in secular music, as may be evidenced from an imperfect copy of 'Hugh Ashton's Maske ', now in the Manuscript Collection of Christ Church, Oxford (Arkwright's *Catalogue*, part 1, 1915).

Of the birth and early education of Whytbroke no particulars whatever have come down, but we find him at Cardinal College, Oxford, in 1525—a contemporary of Taverner—and he was ordained a priest in 1529/30. At this date he must have exhibited musical powers of no mean order, for in May 1530 Dean Higden, of Cardinal College, entrusted him with the delicate mission of investigating the reported encomiums on a Mr. Benbow, who was

---

[1] See *Tudor Church Music*, vol. iii, p. 35.
[2] Whytbroke's Magnificat (edited by Burgess and Shore) has been issued as No. 898 of Novello's Parish Choir Book.

a candidate for the post of Master of the Choristers, in succession to John Taverner. From the *Calendar of Letters and Papers of Henry VIII* we learn that Whytbroke was sent to Manchester to report on the fitness of John Benbow, and, if suitable, to bring him to Oxford. Evidently Whytbroke's report was favourable, for on May 29 of that year, among the items of expenses in the household books of Cardinal College appears the following :

> To Benbowe coming from Manchester to be Master of the Choristers, 29 May, 2*s*. 9*d*.
>
> Expenses of Dom Whytbroke riding for Benbow at the Dean's command, 6*s*. 8*d*.

On the suppression of Cardinal College, Whytbroke's services were rewarded by the important appointment of the sub-deanery of St. Paul's Cathedral, a post almost invariably bestowed on a musical cleric. From the official records we learn that on June 29, 1531, William Whytbroke was presented to the post of sub-dean of St. Paul's Cathedral, being also appointed Vicar of All Saints', Stanton, Suffolk, with licence for more residences. Apropos this latter appointment, there is an interesting note in a manuscript in the British Museum (Add. MSS. 5813, f. 93) which says that Whytbroke ' does not reside at his vicarage, and is not a graduate '. No doubt he had the influential support of Thomas Cromwell, and that was sufficient to satisfy any objections.

The next notice of Whytbroke is his name appended to the ' Declaration of the sub-dean and Canons of St. Paul's Cathedral of allegiance to King Henry VIII and Queen Anne Boleyn, and that the Bishop of Rome has no authority in this Kingdom ' (June 30, 1534). This document was not signed by the dean, Richard Pace, nor by any of the canons, though doubtless the Declaration was capable of meaning the temporal authority of the Pope, and as such could lawfully be signed by orthodox Catholics. The first four names appear as follows:

> Wilhelmus Whytbroke, *Sub-decanus* ; Johannes Smyth, *Cardinalis* ; Thomas Balgay, *Cardinalis* ; and Johannes Haward, *Succentor*.

William Whytbroke

In the document as calendared no names are given—merely the numbers, thus:

> 8 canons, sub-dean and 2 cardinals, 1 succentor, 6 minor canons, 31 *chanters*, and 29 others.

Through the courtesy of my friend, Mr. J. M. Rigg, I was able to obtain a copy of the original Declaration, giving all the names. I may add that the translation of *chanters* for *cantharistae* is not correct: cantarista is a *chantry priest*, not a chanter.

Whytbroke resigned the post of sub-dean of St. Paul's in 1535, and was succeeded by Robert Astlyn, minor canon, while Richard Sampson, who had replaced Dean Pace, was appointed Bishop of Chichester in June 1536. It would seem that he retired to his vicarage of All Saints', Stanton, and spent the remainder of his days quietly.

His setting of the Magnificat in John Day's *Certaine Notes* (1560) is highly prized; but it is well to note that the English adaptation clearly points to the fact that it was originally composed to Latin words. The music would seem to be of the same period of composition as Whytbroke's beautiful Mass, 'Upon the square'—that is, in four parts, as Mr. Barclay Squire explains —a term also used by William Mundy for two of his Masses. He wrote a Latin Magnificat for six voices, of which only the contratenor has survived, and is now in the Bodleian Mus. School, e. 423. Somehow, I hardly imagine that Whytbroke lived as late as 1561, and all the music by him that I have traced bears evidence of a period twenty years earlier. He was a contemporary of John Shepherd, who is said to have died in 1561, and was also of the same period as Hake, Ockland, Johnson, Redford, Ludford, W. Parsons, Alcock, and Gwynneth.

In the Library of Peterhouse, Cambridge, there is a Motet by Whytbroke, probably dating from about the year 1535. It is entitled 'Sancte Deus', set for five voices, and is included in Dr. Jebb's catalogue printed in the *Ecclesiologist* for 1859.

XXV. *Thomas Knight*

IN the course of an interesting article on 'The Early Harmonized Chants of the Church of England', by Mr. Royle Shore (*Musical Times*, September, October, and November 1912), the statement is made that nothing is apparently known of Whytbroke and Knight, whose settings of the Evening Canticles were published by John Day in his *Certaine Notes* (1560). This statement merely echoes the information to be found in most works of reference, and although Knight's compositions are known to students of the Tudor period, no memoir of him has previously appeared. Not even his Christian name has been determined on, and, as a fact, his beautiful Magnificat has recently been published merely with the surname 'Knight', as a Nunc dimittis.

The late Dr. Jebb, in his interesting Catalogue of the Peterhouse Musical MSS., published in the *Ecclesiologist* (vol. xx, 1859), called attention to the compositions by Knight, but was unable to differentiate between Robert Knight and Thomas Knight. Knight's Mass is in the Peterhouse MS. As will be seen later on, it is a mistake to suppose that Thomas Knight lived as late as 1559, and, so far as can be ascertained, all his creative work may safely be assigned to the second quarter of the sixteenth century. As to his relationship with Robert Knight, whose Latin Motet for five voices, 'Propterea maestum', is in the musical library of Peterhouse (Cambridge), I have not been able to trace any connexion, though probably they were contemporary.

In the previous chapter I have shown that William Whytbroke's period of creative activity was between the years 1525 and 1535; but Thomas Knight was of slightly later date, probably between 1530 and 1540. The appearance of his Magnificat in Day's *Certaine Notes* (1560) has been regarded as a proof that Thomas Knight was still alive at that date (1560); yet, as has been shown previously, many of the settings in this rare collection

Thomas Knight

were merely English adaptations of the original Latin texts, and, as a matter of fact, his name is included in Day's publication of 1565.

Without further prelude we may proceed to give some definite facts in the career of Thomas Knight. His date of birth and his early training have not been placed on record. He graduated B.A. at Oxford, June 27, 1530, and M.A. June 19, 1534. We meet with him in 1535 as organist and vicar-choral of Salisbury Cathedral. One thing is certain, that in 1536, among the varied items of the Treasurer's Accounts, there is a sum of 6s. 8d. entered as paid to Thomas Knight for a quarter's salary as organist. The next entry runs as follows : ' Paid Thos. Knyght for playing the Organ, his salary for the quarter, 6s. 8d.' This would be at the munificent rate of £1 6s. 8d. a year ! Yet, as is well known, this yearly salary would be equal to about £12 a year of our present computation. However, it is only fair to point out that this yearly stipend was only a sort of bonus given to Knight in addition to his salary as vicar-choral. As a matter of fact, there was not then—nor for some years later—any recognized organist as such, as the vicars-choral had long been accustomed to take their turn in playing the organ, receiving a certain honorarium.

The next definite item of information concerning Thomas Knight is in 1539, in which year he received a honorarium for acting as organist during Whit-week. The wording of the entry from the Treasurer's Accounts is sufficiently definite : ' Thos. Knyght for playing the Organ in the week of Pentecost, 2s.' Thus we are tolerably certain in describing Knight as vicar-choral and acting-organist of Salisbury Cathedral [1] from 1535 to 1540, and probably till 1545.

Strange to say, the earliest name on the list of official organists of Salisbury Cathedral in Mr. John E. West's valuable book, *Cathedral Organists*, is that of John Farrant, in 1598 ; but it may be noted that Richard Fuller had been organist from 1595 to

---

[1] His successor, ' Sir ' Beckwith, also acted as organist, and received 26s. 8d. ' for playing the organ for the whole year '.

1598. No doubt lay-clerks acted as organists up to about the year 1590.

Nicholas Shaxton, who had been the schismatic Bishop of Salisbury from 1535 to 1539, fell into disgrace, but was pardoned by the King on July 13, 1546, having recanted his errors and dismissed his wife. It is not known whether Thomas Knight continued at Salisbury after the year 1540, but I have found no further mention of his name. The Pope appointed Cardinal Contarini as Bishop on July 23, 1539, but the King's nominee, John Salcot, *alias* Capon, held the temporalities till 1554.

I am strongly of opinion that the Thomas Knight who was granted an annuity out of the dissolved monastery of Spalding in 1545/6 may be identified as the composer of that name. He is still credited as an annuitant of the said monastery in the accounts of 1546/7, as appears from the *Calendar of Letters and Papers of Henry VIII* (vol. xxi, part 2, p. 443).

With this entry of 1546/7 Thomas Knight disappears from history, although further research may bring to light other biographical data concerning him. It is gratifying to add that Mr. Royle Shore has popularized Knight's beautiful Magnificat in his adapted version, issued as No. 898 of Novello's Parish Choir Book.

XXVI.   *John Redford*

Iᴛ is generally admitted that John Redford was not only a remarkable organist, choirmaster, and composer, but also a playwright of distinction under Henry VIII ; yet his biography is a blank so far as our accredited musical historians are concerned. The only information concerning his personality in the second edition of *Grove* is the comparatively vague statement that he was ' Organist and Almoner and Master of the Choristers of St. Paul's Cathedral in the latter part of the reign of Henry VIII '. This is the accepted account of Redford, and strange to say modern investigators acquiesce in placing Redford as flourishing in the ' latter part ' of Henry VIII's reign, that is to say, as flourishing between the years 1530–47.   The only other item of biography vouchsafed is that Tusser was a pupil of Redford. Now it is fairly certain that Tusser's career as a choirboy of St. Paul's cannot have been after 1542 or 1543, and there is no clear evidence that Redford lived much later than 1543. Professor Pollard tells us that Redford's Interlude of ' Wyt and Science ' was written ' probably towards the end of the reign of Henry VIII ', that is, *circa* 1544 ; yet there is ample testimony to show that this date must be placed as *circa* 1538 or 1539. Dr. Ernest Walker, in his *History of Music in England* (1907), confesses that he knows nothing of the life of Redford save that he was organist of St. Paul's Cathedral ' about the middle of the sixteenth century ', and Mr. H. Orsmond Anderton, in his *Early English Music* (1920), suggests that Redford's life ' probably extended from 1491 to 1547 ', but gives no further particulars.

No better proof of Redford's powers need be adduced than the inclusion of his name by Morley, in his *Plaine and Easie Introduction to Practicall Musicke* (1597), among the celebrated English composers who flourished under Henry VIII.   Still stronger proof may be found in the dozens of Redford's compositions preserved in the British Museum, including his beautiful Organ Fantasias, and his Interlude of ' Wyt and Science '. Yet, notwithstanding all his known manuscripts, no serious endeavour has hitherto been made to piece together any facts of his biography. On this account the new light I have been enabled to throw on the career of Redford will be a help to future investigators.

But first I may explain that the name of our distinguished musician will not be found in the printed *Calendar of the Letters and Papers of Henry VIII*, although I have carefully gone through the thirty-five volumes of that monumental work. Yet, as will be seen, it was an entry in vol. 7, in connexion with the year 1534, that supplied me with the hint whereby I was enabled to trace Redford as a Vicar-Choral of St. Paul's Cathedral.

John Redford was born about the year 1486, and was trained in the choir school of St. Paul's Cathedral, ultimately becoming a Vicar-Choral. He was subsequently Organist and Almoner and Master of the Choristers, but in these appointments we do not meet with him until the year 1530. So far as my researches go, it is safe to state that Redford was Organist of St. Paul's from 1525, being also Junior Vicar-Choral, and that he subsequently was appointed Master of the Choristers (1532).

One of the duties of the choirmaster of St. Paul's was to prepare choirboy plays, and we find, from the *Calendar of Papers of Henry VIII*, that on November 10, 1527, ' the children of Paules ' presented at Greenwich, among the Court revels, a Latin-French play, for the entertainment of the French nobles. Cavendish describes it as ' a most godliest disguising or interlude made in Latin and French ', under Master John Rightwise [1].

In a previous article we have seen that, on June 29, 1531, William Whytbroke was appointed Sub-Dean of St. Paul's Cathedral (of which the Dean, Richard Pace, was an excellent musician), and in 1532 he got John Redford appointed almoner and master of the choristers. No wonder, then, that in the ' declaration by the Sub-Dean and Canons of St. Paul's of allegiance to Henry VIII and Queen Anne Boleyn ', on June 20, 1534,

---

[1] John Rightwise was appointed Usher of St. Paul's School under William Lyly in 1510, and succeeded Lyly as Master.

with the pregnant passage that ' the Bishop of Rome has no authority in this Kingdom ', the names of Whytbroke and Redford appear. This interesting document is signed by the sub-dean, eight canons, two cardinals, one succentor, six minor canons, thirty-one chantry priests, and twenty-three others.[1] None of the names is given in the printed Calendar, but through the courtesy of Mr. J. M. Rigg, of the Public Record Office, I obtained the exact transcript of all the signatures in the original document, including Whytbroke, Hayward (succentor), John Smyth and Thos. Balgrave (cardinals), and the following vicars-choral : William Sampton, Bartholomew Ody, Robert Pate, Thomas Baldwin, *John Redford*, and John Purvoche.

Let it not be supposed that this Declaration indicated a change of religion ; it was merely a loyal formality in which the temporal power of the Pope was denied. Anyhow, many of those that signed it were taken into Court favour, and Redford was in high repute as a choirmaster as well as organist. At the close of 1534, or early in 1535, the famous Thomas Tusser was, ' by friend-ship's lot ', taken into the choir school of St. Paul's, a proceeding which rescued him from being impressed, or conscripted, by roaming choir agents, who had ' placards ' for taking up suitable choristers. Tusser thus eulogizes Redford in his *One Hundred Points of Good Husbandry* [2], published in 1557 :

> But mark the chance, myself to vance
> By friendship's lot to Paul's I got,
> So found I grace a certain space
>   Still to remain.
> With REDFORD there, the like no where,
> For cunning such and virtue much
> By whom some part of music's art,
>   So did I gain.

---

[1] The printed Calendar gives ' 29 others ', but the actual number was only twenty-three, as the list included the six vicars-choral. The Calendar also mistranslates ' cantarista ' as ' chanters '.

[2] This title developed into ' Five Hundred Points ' in 1573.

Early Tudor Composers

Richard Sampson, Bishop of Chichester, whose career has been described in Chapter XXII, was Dean of St. Paul's from July 1536 (in succession to Dean Pace), and was a friend to Redford. On October 13, 1537, there was a grand 'Te Deum' sung in St. Paul's under Redford's direction, for the birth of Prince Edward.

There is no other incident chronicled in respect of this remarkable musician until 1538/9, when his Interlude of 'Wyt and Science' was performed. The date of this Interlude has been given by all previous writers as between the years 1541 and 1546; yet, as the proof rested on the introduction of the Galliard into England, I venture to assert that Redford's play must be dated as of the year 1538 or early in 1539. For proof of this the reader is referred to a communication of mine in *The Times Literary Supplement* (March 3, 1921). Professor Wallace tells us that Redford was a great friend of John Heywood, seven of whose songs he had collected in a volume, with musical setting.

In the Interlude are three songs set to music by Redford, namely, 'Give place, give place, to honest recreation', 'Exceeding measure with pains continual', and 'Welcome, mine own'. At the end is written, 'Here cometh in four with viols and sing "remembrance", and at the last quere [verse] all make curtesy and so go forth singing'. As customary, the final prayer is for the King and Queen: 'Thus endeth the play of "Wyt and Science", made by Master John Redford.'

After the year 1540 there is no trace of Redford, and it seems likely that he died in that year or the year following. Probably he was succeeded by Thomas Mulliner, but of this I have discovered no proof. Redford's anthem, 'Rejoice in the Lord alway', is still sung at St. Paul's, and an octavo edition by the late Sir George Martin was published by Messrs. Novello in 1894. His organ solo, 'Glorificamus' (Add. MSS. Brit. Mus. 30513) has been edited by Mr. John E. West for the same publishers.

From the carefully compiled 'Catalogue of Manuscript Music in the Library of Christ Church, Oxford' (1915), by Mr. G. E. P. Arkwright, we learn that there are three volumes by Redford in

John Redford

the Library, namely, a Motet ('Vestri precincti') for six voices (wanting the tenor part), a Voluntary for organ, and five Organ pieces.

But the great bulk of Redford's work lies interned in the British Museum, including his sacred song, 'Walking alone' (Add. MSS. 15233), and his 'Christus Resurgens', in two sections for four voices (Add. MSS. 17802–17805)[1]. His Interlude of 'Wyt and Science' (*circa* 1538) deserves to be better known, and it is of interest to note that this musical play ends with a prayer for the King and Queen, a convention that continued for two centuries, and that ultimately developed into the playing of the National Anthem.

No doubt the best of Redford's compositions will shortly occupy the attention of the responsible committee of the Carnegie Trust, and will, at no distant date, be available for students of early Tudor music.

[1] Mr. H. B. Collins suggests that Byrd in his 'Gradualia' took Redford's setting as his model.

XXVII. *Thomas Appleby*

CONSIDERING that there are Masses, Magnificats, and Motets by
Thomas Appleby—all of a good quality—it is surprising that his
biography has hitherto proved so elusive. Even the new edition
of Henry Davey's *History of English Music* (1921) dismisses his
career in one sentence: 'Thomas Appleby also appears in the
latter set of part-books; he was organist of Magdalen College,
Oxford, in 1539.' It is almost needless to add that neither Burney
nor Hawkins throws any light on this remarkable organist and composer. Fortunately, the publication of the valuable *Lincoln
Chapter Records*, admirably edited by Canon Cole, affords us much
desired information as to Appleby, who was for two periods
organist and Master of the Choristers of Lincoln Cathedral.
I take this opportunity, also, for expressing my sincere thanks to
Canon Cole for his kindness in forwarding me the transcripts of
all the Chapter Acts bearing on musical appointments from 1520
to 1560.

The name of this Tudor musician appears variously as Appleby,
Appelby, and Appulby, but it will be more convenient to adhere
to the spelling 'Appleby'. He was probably a native of Lincoln,
born 1498, and educated as a chorister in the Cathedral, afterwards proceeding to Oxford. Thomas Appleby, of Balliol College;
supplicated B.A., April 26, 1510; admitted May 2; licensed for
M.A., June 27, 1515. Be this as it may, he must have displayed
unusual musical ability, and at the age of thirty-eight he appears
as acting-organist of Lincoln Cathedral in 1536, owing to the
ill-health of Robert Dove, Vicar-Choral[1]. According to the
Chapter Records, the said Dove received but 40s. for playing the
organ at the Mass of the Blessed Virgin, and 20s. 8d. for playing

---

[1] A namesake, Thomas Appleby, was Vicar of Braintree in 1535.

at the Jesus Mass. His death took place in April 1537, whereupon Thomas Appleby was provisionally appointed his successor.

A Thomas Appleby, chaplain, on June 21, 1509, was granted the perpetual chantry of St. Margaret within Barnard Castle, and on May 16 following the hermitage and chapel of St. Mary Magdalene within the parish of Gainforth, diocese of Durham. He resigned the chapelry in Barnard Castle in January 1522, and was succeeded by Christopher Appulby, February 19, 1522. This, however, is not our composer.

By a Chapter Act of April 23, 1538, Appleby was confirmed in the joint-offices of organist and Master of the Choristers of Lincoln. However, he held the position only for a little over a year, as in July 1539 he was induced to take the post of organist of Magdalen College, Oxford, being replaced at Lincoln by James Crawe in the joint-offices of organist and ' Master of the Song ', with the salary and fees attaching to both offices, and with a gratuity of 13*s.* 4*d.* annually on condition that during his life he, or his deputy, ' shall duly and diligently instruct and teach the choristers both in the science of singing, namely, plainsong, pricked song, faburden, discant, and counterpoint, as well as playing the organ ', also teaching certain apt choirboys ' to play on the instruments called Clavichords, said boys to provide Clavichords at their own proper cost and expense '. These Letters Patent of James Crawe are dated October 4, 1539.

Two years later Thomas Appleby returned to Lincoln (being replaced at Magdalen College by John Sheppard), and on November 21, 1541, his Letters Patent were drawn up in somewhat the same form as those of James Crawe. In the Chapter Act it is stated that the said Thomas Appleby was unanimously reappointed to the joint positions ' vacant by the dismission of Master James Crawe ', and that, as a mark of favour, he was to be given a suitable chamber ' situated over the outer gate of the Choristers' House '.

Evidently Appleby must have given satisfaction to the Chapter, because he held his post during the remaining years of Henry VIII, and also under Edward VI and Queen Mary, although adhering

to the ancient faith. The following extract from a Chapter Act
of February 12, 1558/9, testifies to the esteem in which he was
held :

> On 12 Feb., 1558, the Sub-dean and Chapter, assembled
> chapterwise, for the good and faithful service rendered by
> Thomas Appleby, skilled in the art of music, unanimously
> granted to him the office of Seneschal or Procurator of the
> House of Choristers, and Collector of all farms, payments,
> and emoluments belonging to them, immediately after the
> death, dismission, &c., of Thomas Paget, the present Seneschal,
> to be held during their good pleasure.

Six months later, on August 18, 1559, we learn from the Chapter
Acts that Thomas Appleby ' was admitted to the office of Seneschal
of the Choristers, vacant by the dismission of Thomas Paget,
according to a certain grant made to Thos. Appleby by the
Chapter '.

' Dismission ' evidently meant ' resignation ', for, on the same
day, Thomas Paget, Seneschal, was appointed to the office of
Sacrist, being also admitted Vicar-Choral.

Appleby was now an old man, and though he still played the
organ, the Precentor relieved him of the duty of teaching the
choristers. This we learn from a Chapter Act of September 19,
1559, when Roger Dalison, Precentor, was appointed ' Master
and Supervisor of the Choristers, poor clerks, and boys in the
foundation of Bartholomew Burgherse '.

I have failed to meet with any record of Appleby after the year
1560, and evidently he died at the close of the year 1562, as in
February 1563 the illustrious William Byrd was appointed his
successor. Through the courtesy of Canon Johnston, Chancellor
of Lincoln Cathedral, I am enabled to give the exact date when
Byrd was officially appointed in place of Appleby, a date unknown
to previous investigators, although the usual authorities give us
' about the year 1563 '. From the Chapter Acts the date of
Byrd's appointment to Lincoln is given as February 27, 1562/3,
when the composer was in his twenty-first year.

Thomas Appleby

Appleby's compositions may be dated as between the years 1530–50, and though, doubtless, many of them have been lost, sufficient remain to appraise his merits. The Peterhouse MSS. contain a Mass and a Magnificat by him, while the British Museum Add. MSS. 17802–5 include a fine Mass. It does not appear that he composed anything for the English Service, and in fact his creative period was long before the reign of Elizabeth. His twenty-one years' connexion with Lincoln continued the good tradition established by Thomas Ashwell, which was developed by his successor, Byrd.

XXVIII.　*John Dygon*

Among the few early Tudor composers whose works are quoted by Sir John Hawkins the name of John Dygon has an honoured place. Hawkins printed a Motet of his from the Royal Collection, namely, 'Ad lapidis positionem', but so little did the great English musical historian know of Dygon's biography that he considered the work as having been composed towards the middle of the sixteenth century.

Since Hawkins's day no new light has been thrown on the career of Dygon save that he graduated Mus.Bac. at Oxford in 1512, and that he was Prior of St. Augustine's Abbey, Canterbury, at the dissolution of the monasteries in 1538. Neither Dr. Ernest Walker nor Mr. Henry Davey has pierced the obscurity which has hitherto enveloped Dygon's biography, and though the amount of new information which I have gleaned is not so large as could be desired, yet the facts now brought to light may serve to stimulate some future delver of Tudor records.

John Dygon was a nephew of the John Dygon who was elected Abbot of St. Augustine's, Canterbury, in January 1497, and was a novice under his uncle between the years 1497 and 1504. It is safe to assume that he was born *circa* 1485, and he doubtless entered the famous Canterbury choristers' school in 1494. This choristers' school had been endowed so far back as February 1319/20, by Prior Henry, of Eastry, and had therefore a good tradition. Young Dygon, after his reception as a novice, displayed uncommon musical abilities, and at length, having supplicated on March 28, 1512, he was granted the degree of Mus.Bac. at Oxford.

Meantime, Dygon's uncle died in 1509, and was succeeded as Abbot by John Hampton, after whom came John Vokes (Essex). A curious hypothesis was started by Mr. A. Hughes-Hughes in his article on Dygon in the new edition of Grove's *Dictionary of*

John Dygon

Music and Musicians to the effect that John Dygon was probably an *alias* or assumed name for John Wyldebere, or else that he was to be identified with John Wilborne, who was alive in 1557.

Fortunately, there is no need for this complex hypothesis as to the identity of John Dygon, because we learn from John Twyne, the famous antiquary, who was schoolmaster in the Canterbury school and was a friend of John Vokes, last Abbot of St. Augustine's (whose rule extended from 1521 to 1538), that the Abbot ' sent John Dygon, sub-prior of the monastery, to Louvain ', in 1521, in order to avail of the tuition of the celebrated Juan Luis Vives, the Spanish humanist. In 1521 Will. Selling was Precentor of St. Augustine's, Canterbury.

Dygon studied under Vives, who had been a Fellow of Corpus in 1517, at Louvain from 1521 to 1523, and then returned to England with his master, who had been urged to take up the post of Lecturer on Rhetoric in Oxford University by Cardinal Wolsey. As is well known, Vives came over, and resided at Corpus Christi College, then under the presidency of Dr. John Claymond. On October 10, 1523, he supplicated for incorporation. So great was his fame that he attracted vast numbers to his lectures, including Henry VIII and Queen Katherine, being also appointed tutor to the Princess Mary (1524–6). Two other distinguished scholars had come over with John Dygon and Vives, namely, Nicholas Wotton and Jerome Ruffaldus, in 1523.

Not alone the antiquary Twyne but Vives himself has borne ample testimony to the outstanding abilities of Dygon. Vives mentions him with eulogy, nay, ' with great affection ', as Cardinal Gasquet writes (*The Eve of the Reformation*, p. 38). Dr. Nicholas Wotton was made Dean of the Chapel of the Princess Mary. He was afterwards an ambassador, and Jerome Ruffaldus subsequently became Abbot of St. Vaast, Arras.

So great were the merits of Dygon both as a musician and a learned monk that Abbot Vokes, in 1528, promoted him to be Prior of St. Augustine's. Meantime, his friend Vives had married Margaret Valdanra at Bruges, in 1524, but he returned to England on October 1, 1528.

Early Tudor Composers

Dygon continued as Prior of St. Augustine's from 1528 to 1538, and on July 13, 1533, was admitted B.C.L. of Oxford. He was also schoolmaster of the Almonry School (which had been confirmed by a Bull of Pope Eugene IV, dated December 28, 1431). At length came the dissolution of this famous Abbey, when Abbot, Prior, monks, and Song School had all to disappear. The deed of ' Surrender ' is dated July 30, 1538, and the first two signatures are those of the Abbot and Prior, namely, John Essex and John Dygon. The late Dr. James Gairdner in his *Lollardy and the Reformation* (1908) caustically writes that Henry VIII had been guilty of many villainies, including ' the plunder of St. Augustine's monastery, from which he turned out the monks, and put deer in their places '.

In the list of pensions granted to the monks of St. Augustine's, Canterbury, on September 2, 1538, the Abbot and Prior were assigned substantial amounts. Abbot Vokes did not long survive his deprivation, as his death took place in January 1541, but John Dygon is believed to have become secularized and to have assumed the name of John Wilbore. Mr. A. Hughes-Hughes says that ' there is good reason for believing that he was the John Wylbore who was appointed prebendary of Rochester Cathedral in 1541, and who died there in 1553 '.

Anyhow, John Dygon, Mus.Bac., Prior of St. Augustine's, was assigned the pension of £13 6s. 8d., and as such disappears, but if we assume that he adopted the name of Wilbore, there is some reason to agree with the view of Mr. Hughes-Hughes, as, in the new constitution of Rochester Cathedral on June 18, 1541, Hugh ap Rice was appointed first Prebendary, John Wilbore second Prebendary, and Robert Johnson third Prebendary, with Walter Phillips as Dean. All the same, I have a shrewd suspicion that John Dygon's name was his own, and if so, unless he adopted an *alias*, he disappears from the records in 1538. His master, Juan Luis Vives, had been imprisoned for espousing the cause of Queen Katherine over the divorce question, and died on May 30, 1540. It is not at all improbable that Dygon also died before the close of the year 1541, if not earlier, and he was known only by the

106

John Dygon

name of John Dygon to such intimate friends as Vives and the antiquary Twyne : in fact, the authority of the latter, who was a contemporary, goes far to disprove the ingenious suggestion of Mr. Hughes-Hughes as to Dygon's change of name.

Unfortunately most of the compositions of Dygon have disappeared, but sufficient remain to attest his powers. In particular his beautiful three-part Motet, ' Ad lapidis positionem ', and his ' Rex benedicte ', now in Buckingham Palace, stamp him as attempting higher flights than most of the English Tudor school of the period 1500–20. Mr. Hughes-Hughes thinks that this Motet ' bears some resemblance in style to the music of Okeghem, as was very natural, considering how nearly contemporary the two composers were ', but it must be borne in mind that Okeghem wrote between the years 1453–83, whereas Dygon was not born till 1490. Further, Mr. Hughes-Hughes says that ' some passages bear a comparatively modern stamp, and one can detect a foreshadowing of Giovanni Croce, and even of a still later style in several places '. I cannot agree with this opinion, as assuredly Dygon's style is very far removed from that of Croce. Yet Dygon's work is really good for the period, and does not deserve the harsh verdict passed on it by Dr. Ernest Walker.

XXIX. *John Gwynneth, Mus.Doc.*

REGARDING this distinguished Tudor composer the biographical data are very scant. Even Davey thus dismisses him :

> Gwynneth, a secular priest, was presented to a London vicarage—St. Peter's, Cheap—in 1543 ; he resigned in the reign of Mary, when he published tracts against the Protestants. His only known work is the song in Wynkyn de Worde's book.

He adds that Gwynneth ' was licensed to proceed Mus.Doc., Oxon., in 1531 ', and quotes Anthony à Wood's remarks.

Considering that Gwynneth is included in Anthony à Wood's list of famous Oxford composers, as well as in Morley's oft-quoted list, and that he is mentioned by Dr. Burney, it is strange that his biography has never been adequately explored by English musicologists. The inclusion of his song, ' My love mourneth ', for four voices, in Wynkyn de Worde's printed Song-Book, dated October 10, 1530, is ample proof of his reputation as a composer at that date.

From the *Register of the University of Oxford* we learn that John Gwynneth, on supplicating for the degree of Mus.D. on December 9, 1531, set forth that he

> . . . had composed all the Responses for the year, *in cantis crispis aut fractis, ut aiunt,* and many Masses, including three Masses of 5 parts, and five Masses of 4 parts, as well as Hymns, Antiphons, &c.

Evidently his abilities must have been recognized, for we read that he was licensed to graduate as Doctor of Music on payment of a fee of 20*d*. (*Oxford Register,* i. 167).

John Gwynneth was born *circa* 1498, and was an exhibitioner

John Gwynneth, Mus.Doc.

of Oxford. In 1527 he was an acolyte, and in 1530 was presented to the Rectory of the Free Chapel of Stokesbury (Northampton). A few years later he indulged in controversial matters of religion, and in 1536 he published the first part of his treatise against Frith's book—that is, the Book against the Sacraments, denying Transubstantiation, written by John Frith, who was executed for heresy, under Henry VIII, on July 4, 1533, together with Andrew Hewet, a tailor's apprentice (Gairdner's *Lollardy and the Reformation*, i. 415). Contrary to the general view, it is well to note that Frith was given every opportunity to recant, but refused, even at the request of Cranmer.

On September 1, 1534, John Gwynneth, clerk, was presented to a collegiate church in the diocese of Bath and Wells (*Cal. Lett. Hen. VIII*, vol. viii). Two years later, on August 20, 1536, the name of John Gwynneth, chaplain, appears in certain depositions against Dom Wm. Ashwell (ibid., vol. xi). About this time he composed some Motets, now in the Pepysian Library, Magdalene College, Cambridge.

From official records it appears that on October 22, 1537, John Gwynneth, Mus.D., was presented to the Provostship of Clynnog Vaur, diocese of Bangor, *vice* William Glynne, deceased. Further preferment, however, awaited him, as on September 19, 1543, he was appointed Rector of St. Peter's, Cheapside ; but a difficulty arose, as the versatile clerical musician was anxious to retain his post at Clynnog Vaur. In 1544 and 1545 litigation went on, and at length, on January 7, 1546, a friend of his at Court, Stephen Vaughan, suggested that

> . . . as John Gwynneth had, after eight years' protracted suit, recovered the said Provostship of Clevok Vawre for the King, it might revert to the King as a chantry, and Gwynneth might be permitted to retain it.

In this letter it is stated that Gwynneth was also Vicar of Luton, and he was 'a brother to Vaughan's deceased wife', and that his suit over the Provostship 'had cost him above 500 marks' (*Cal. Lett. Hen. VIII*, vol. xxi).

Early Tudor Composers

The next we hear of Gwynneth is in 1556, under Queen Mary, when he resigned his Rectory of St. Peter's, Cheapside (also known as West Cheap, or simply ' Cheap ')—a stately church that disappeared in the Great Fire of London and was never rebuilt. Between the years 1543 and 1556 he had done much to keep up a good standard of music in his church, and had availed himself of the services of Father Howe to repair the ' organs ' and ' regals ', as well as paying him his fee for ' keeping the organs ' (*Church-wardens' Accounts*, edited by Rev. W. Sparrow Simpson, 1868).

Gwynneth lived for some years after his resignation, as he was certainly alive in 1561–2 ; but doubtless he had to live in retirement owing to the change of religion, as he stood openly by the old faith. His niece, Jane Vaughan—daughter of Cuthbert Vaughan—married Thomas Wiseman, eldest son and heir of John Wiseman, of Felsted, and of Braddocks (Broad Oaks), Essex (died January 5, 1568). She was condemned, on July 3, 1598, to be pressed to death, for having harboured a Roman Catholic priest. Though reprieved by Queen Elizabeth, she yet had to remain in prison till 1603, when she was released. She died in 1610. Strange to say, Mrs. Wiseman's brother-in-law, Ralph Wiseman, was knighted in 1608, as was also her son, Sir William Wiseman. Lady readers may be interested to learn that this Jane Vaughan, ' of an ancient and noble family in Wales, had been sought in marriage by thirty suitors ', but preferred Thomas Wiseman. In her house she kept John Bolt, *alias* Johnson, who had been a Court musician and in favour with Queen Elizabeth (see his memoir in Grove's *Dictionary of Music*), and whose life was spared owing to the influence of Penelope Lady Rich in 1594.

From the *Chronicle of St. Monica's, Louvain* (edited by Dom A. Hamilton, O.S.B., 1904), we learn that John Gwynneth had suffered imprisonment in the first years of Elizabeth's reign, and he it was who arranged the marriage of his niece, Jane Vaughan, to Thomas Wiseman. Here is the quaint narrative :

> Her uncle by the mother's side, named Mr. Gwynneth, who was a priest and had been rector of a parish church in

110

John Gwynneth, Mus.Doc.

London in Catholic times, could not assist her in all so well as he desired, being a long time kept in prison when heresy came in. But at length getting freedom (*circa* 1561–2) he was desirous to match this his niece worthily, and as should be best for her soul's good. Whereupon, one day he met with Mr. Wiseman, a young gentleman of the Inns of Court, and liked him so well that, upon the proposition of one in the company, he became content to marry his niece with him, and brought him unto her, persuading her, if she could like him, to take him for her husband. But she was ever very backward in that matter, insomuch that having no less than thirty suitors, some whereof had seven years sought her goodwill, yet she should not settle her love upon any. But now it was God's Will that she should yield herein to her uncle, and so was married to Mr. Wiseman, who brought her home to his house in Essex, when she found both father and mother-in-law and a household of brothers and sisters.

As the marriage of Gwynneth's niece took place in 1561–2, we must assume (from the *Chronicle*) that the priest-composer was alive at that date, but he probably died soon after. His fame mainly rests on the printed part-song of 1530, for which he supplied words as well as music, but he is also included in Morley's list of distinguished Old English composers, in his *Plaine and Easie Introduction to Practicall Musicke* (1597), where his name appears as ' Jo. Guinneth '. His creative period as a musician may safely be dated between the years 1525 and 1555.

XXX. *Richard Edwards*

In 1567 Dr. Thomas Twyne (Fellow of Corpus Christi College, Oxford, in 1564) wrote a lengthy and eulogistic epitaph on Richard Edwards, describing him as ' the flower of all our realm and Phoenix of our age '. His musical powers are thus alluded to :

> Thy tender tunes and rimes wherein thou wontest to play,
> Each princely dame of Court and town shall bear in mind alway.

But Edwards is immortalized by Shakespeare (*Romeo and Juliet*), who quotes his song, ' In Commendation of Musick '; and he is equally immortalized by reason of the words and music of his lovely madrigal, commencing :

> In going to my naked bed, as one that would have slept,
> I heard a wife sing to her child, that long before had wept.

Professor Wallace writes :

> Edwards was by far the best poet that had graced the Court since the days of Cornish, and was his superior in both conception and expression. As lyricist, he was the highest achievement England had yet attained. His songs in manuscript, and those collected under his name in *The Paradise of Dainty Devices*, mellifluous and lilting as bird-music, were such as he sprinkled his plays with, and may generally have been intended for such entertainments. Both as lyricist and dramatist he added glory to the Chapel Royal as a centre of dramatic entertainment, and composed a number of plays or interludes which were acted by the Children before her Majesty (*The Evolution of the English Drama up to Shakespeare*, Berlin, 1912).

Notwithstanding all this praise of Edwards, the biographical details are scanty until about the year 1560, when he was appointed

Richard Edwards

by patent as Gentleman of the Chapel Royal (May 27, 1560)—
the earliest ascertained fact in his career, according to Professor
Wallace. Fortunately, the present writer has succeeded in rescuing from oblivion a few interesting and hitherto unpublished
notices of this remarkable Tudor composer.

Richard Edwards was born near Yeovil, in Somersetshire, about
the year 1522, and was sent to Corpus Christi College, Oxford,
which he entered on May 11, 1540, and had the good fortune to
be placed under Dr. George Etheridge, as tutor—Etheridge being
regarded as ' one of the most excellent vocal and instrumental
musicians in England ' (Pitts), being also an eminent physician
and Greek Professor. After four years' study Edwards became
a Fellow of Corpus Christi College on August 11, 1544, and was
admitted B.A. on November 3 following. However, in 1547, on
the foundation of Christ Church College, he took his Master's
degree there, as is referred to by Dr. Thomas Twyne in his
Epitaph of Master Edwards :

> O happy house ! O place of Corpus Christi, thou
> That plantedst first, and gavest the root to that so beau
> a bow.
> And Christ Church, which enjoyedst the fruit more ripe at
> fill,
> Plunge up a thousand sighs, for grief your trickling tears
> distil.

Curiously enough, in previous accounts of Edwards, there is
a complete blank from 1547 to 1560, and the inference has been
assumed that he did not join the Chapel Royal till 1560. This is
not so, as will be seen ; as a fact, he received livery as a Gentleman of the Chapel Royal at Queen Mary's Coronation in 1554.

From the Register of Oxford University it appears that Edwards
was an Inceptor of Theology on February 6, 1545, and he was
ordained a priest on taking his M.A. in 1547. He was appointed
Perpetual Curate of St. George's, Botolph Lane and George Lane,
London, on September 16, 1549, but resigned that post in 1552
on being presented to the Rectory of St. Helen's, Worcester. Yet

it seems fairly certain that he was a Gentleman of the Chapel Royal under Edward VI in 1552, for doubtless the name ' George Edwards of the Chappell ', to whom a fee was paid in 1552 (Stow MSS., Brit. Mus., 571, f. 36b), is a scribal error for Richard Edwards. In the official list of the Chapel Royal, for the Coronation of Queen Mary, on September 17, 1553, there were thirty-one suits of livery ordered, and among the Gentlemen Richard Edwards appears, with Richard Bowyer as Master of the Children. Probably owing to non-residence, he had to resign the Rectory of St. Helen's, Worcester, on July 12, 1555, as is stated in Bishop Pate's Register, and was succeeded by John Bullingham, who was deprived six months later.

At the accession of Queen Elizabeth, Edwards was given a Coronation livery, and he acted as Deputy-Master of the Children of the Chapel Royal from 1560 to July 26, 1561, when he succeeded Richard Bowyer as Master for life. On December 4, 1561, he received a commission empowering him to impress choristers for the Chapel Royal.

During Queen Mary's short rule Edwards composed a Mass and some Latin Motets, including ' Terrenum sitiens regnum ', the manuscript of which is now at Peterhouse. He also composed ' O the silly man ' (madrigal), an organ version of which is in the Mulliner MS., No. 76, folio 77b. Dr. Fellowes (*English Madrigal Composers*) points out that in this madrigal occurs ' a very early example of the use of the chord of the major third and minor sixth ', the date of which is not later than 1558.

Between the years 1561 and 1563 Edwards and his boys delighted the Court with plays, including ' Appius and Virginius '. These plays were highly praised by Barnaby Gooch in *Eglogs, Epytaphes, and Sonettes*, published on March 15, 1563, who, in commendation of ' Edwardes of the Chapell ', describes his plays as far surpassing Plautus and Terence, and not likely to be equalled by any future poet.

Edwards was admitted a member of Lincoln's Inn on November 25, 1564, and he produced his famous ' new tragical comedy ', entitled ' Damon and Pythias ', for the delectation of the Court during the Christmas revels of 1564–5. Shortly afterwards, on February 2, 1565, the Chapel Royal boys, under Edwards, produced a play said to be 'Misogonus', at Lincoln's Inn, receiving for same 53s. 4d. Exactly a year later he produced another play at the same place, for which he was paid 40s. Then followed, at Christ Church, Oxford, two more 'tragical comedies', under the name of 'Palæmon and Arcyte', on September 2 and September 4, 1566, played by the scholars for the entertainment of Queen Elizabeth. This play vastly delighted the Queen, who sent for Edwards, and 'gave him promise of reward', but it is doubtful if the promise materialized, for the poet-musician sickened soon after, and died on October 31, 1566.

Edwards contributed a setting of the metrical version of the Lord's Prayer to Day's Psalter in 1563, and he composed the music for Surrey's 'Ye happy dames'. Even better known is his song, 'When griping grief' (quoted by Shakespeare), and also his famous 'Soul-knell'. But among all his works the most delightful is the madrigal, 'In going to my naked bed', the words of which were published in his posthumous volume, *The Paradise of Dainty Devices*. By a fortunate circumstance, Mr. H. Elliot Button, early in 1923, discovered manuscript copies (*circa* 1597) of the tenor and bass parts of this madrigal, thus permitting of a more accurate reconstruction of the composition than had previously been possible from the organ score in the Mulliner MS. (British Museum). This reconstructed vocal score was published in the *Musical Times* (July 1923), and the changes are all for the better, bringing out clearly the old-world beauty of Edwards's work.

Let me add that Dr. Etheridge, the tutor of Edwards, described by Henry Davey as 'a stubborn Romanist, who was still alive in 1585', was Regius Professor of Greek at Oxford and a sound musician.

XXXI. *Edward Higgins*

ALTHOUGH it is known that Edward Higgins composed some Masses and Motets in the first quarter of the sixteenth century, yet none of his works have come down to us. However, he deserves inclusion in the present series of articles as the writer of the magnificent full-choir book now in Caius College, Cambridge, known as the Gonville and Caius College MS. 667—a really splendid parchment measuring 28 in. by 20 in. At the end of the manuscript is written, ' Ex dono et opere Eduardi Higgons hujus ecclesie Canonici '.

Strange to say, none of our musical historians could find any clue to the biography of this musical Canon, but Mr. Henry Davey surmises that the Caius MS. was written ' *circa* 1510–20 '. The Right Rev. Dr. Frere is of opinion that the handwriting of this manuscript is the same as that of the famous Lambeth MS., but other experts are not of the same way of thinking. In fact, the tradition of Lambeth is that the manuscript came from St. Albans Abbey, and that the scribe was none other than Dr. Fayrfax himself, whose exercise for his Mus.Doc. is included therein.

Fortunately, my researches have resulted in a goodly number of entries from official sources relating to Higgins, who, as will be seen, was not only a musician, but also a D.C.L. of Oxford, and a Canon of St. Stephen's Chapel Royal, Westminster, and of Lincoln.

Edward Higgins—whose family came from Exeter—was born about the year 1488, and graduated B.C.L. of Oxford in 1507, proceeding to D.C.L. on February 3, 1510/11. On August 1, 1511, he was presented to the Church of Lanteglos-juxta-Stratton (Cornwall), void by the death of Thomas Moreton (Patent Rolls, 3 Henry VIII, p. 1, m. 8). Seven months later (March 9, 1512) he was admitted a Master in Chancery, void by the death of

Edward Higgins

Thomas Cowley. In the letters of admission, directed to the Archbishop of Canterbury, he is described as ' clerk and Councillor '.

On June 7, 1513, Master Edward Higgins, ' King's chaplain ' (who had accompanied King Henry VIII to Thérouanne and Tournai), was granted the Deanery of Shrewsbury, *vice* Master Adam Grafton, resigned, ' a pension of six marks being reserved for the said Adam out of the issues of the Deanery ' (Patent Rolls, 5 Henry VIII, p. 2, m. 15). He resigned this Deanery on May 11, 1517, on his appointment to the Rectory of the Church of Meifod, in the diocese of St. Asaph, but he resigned this benefice in July 1518, on being appointed to a Canonry of St. Stephen's (Chapel Royal), Westminster, on an exchange of benefices with John Vesey, Dean of the Chapel Royal.

If I may be permitted a conjecture as to the date of the famous Caius MS. 667, I would venture to say that Dr. Higgins wrote it between the years 1519 and 1525. In regard to his preferments, it is certain that on July 6, 1522, he was granted the Prebend of St. Stephen's, void by exchange with the celebrated Thomas Linacre, M.D., who had been granted it four months previously. The then Master of the Choristers was Richard Pygot (*vide* above, Chap. VII, pp. 34 *seq.*), while the Dean was John Chambre, M.D., a good musical amateur. Another of his co-Canons was John Stokesley, subsequently Bishop of London.

Further preferment awaited Higgins, who, in 1530, was appointed Master of Arundel Collegiate Church, Sussex. On September 3, 1535, he was appointed a Canon of Lincoln, as appears from the *Valor Ecclesiasticus*. These two appointments he held till his death, which occurred two years later, on January 6, 1537/8.

An old friend has suggested to me that the Caius MS., written by Higgins, was for Lincoln Cathedral, but inasmuch as his appointment to that preferment was not till 1535, such a suggestion must be ruled out, as the manuscript is almost certainly from about the year 1523 or 1524.

It may be well to give a brief summary of the contents of the Caius MS. 667, which, in truth, was a princely gift, apart from the labour of transcription. In all there are ten Masses and five Magnificats. Dr. Fayrfax is represented by five Masses, viz. 'O bone Jesu', 'Regali', 'O quam glorifice', 'Tecum principium', and 'Albanus'; Nicholas Ludford by four, 'Cristi virgo', 'Videte miraculum', 'Benedicta', and 'Lapidaverunt'; William Pasche by one, 'Criste resurgens'. The five Magnificats are by Fayrfax, Cornish, Ludford, Turges, and Trentes. Above all, this manuscript is in almost perfect condition, and, fortunately, the missing leaves can be supplied from the Lambeth MS.

In conclusion, I would express the hope that the Carnegie United Kingdom Trust may give us some day a transcript of both the Lambeth MS. and the Caius MS.

XXXII. *William Parsons*

THERE is considerable confusion over the composers Parsons, as two of the same name were practically contemporaneous. However, William Parsons was evidently of a slightly earlier period, as he flourished under Henry VIII and Queen Mary; Robert Parsons did not come into prominence till 1560.

According to the late Professor Wooldridge, in his article on the 'Psalter' in Grove's *Dictionary*, William Parsons was 'an excellent composer', as is evidenced by his admirable setting of tunes in Day's *Whole Psalmes in foure partes*, published in 1563. This rare publication, in four volumes—of which only a few copies can be traced—contains a hundred and forty-one compositions, of which eighty-one are by Parsons, who seems to have been the editor.

Up to the present, however, notwithstanding the admitted excellence of Parsons's compositions, his biography has been a blank. None of our musical historians could penetrate the veil which hid the life-work of this remarkable Tudor composer, and hence the facts now gleaned may prove of interest if not of permanent value.

William Parsons was born about the year 1515, and he seems to have essayed composition as early as 1536. One thing is certain : there is an interesting Latin Motet of his in a Bodleian MS. (Bodl. e. 423) dating from 1537. Another Motet of his, also in Latin, may be dated as from the year 1546, before the death of Henry VIII.

In 1551 Parsons was engaged by the Dean and Chapter of Wells as assistant-choirmaster and copyist. The then Dean was Dr. William Turner, who had been installed *vice* Dr. John Goodman deprived, and evidently Parsons became an accommodating servant of the 'reformed' Dean. In the Communar's Paper Book of Wells for the year 1551/2 we find that on February 11 the sum of 16s. 4d. was paid to William Parsons 'for divers songs and books by him made and to be made'.

For the year 1552/3 the sum of 12s. was paid to Parsons by the Dean and Chapter of Wells ' for divers songs by him made and to be made '. On August 29, 1553, he was paid 5s. ' for 15 books containing 3 Masses and a Primer ' ; and another significant entry is a payment of 4s. 8d. for ' a book of the Common Prayer for the quyer '.

In 1553, with the advent of Queen Mary, Dr. John Goodman was restored to the Deanery, but was again deprived in 1559, and William Turner was re-installed as Dean. Meantime, like the historic Vicar of Bray, Parsons kept his post at Wells, and in the Communar's Book for 1559/60 there is a fairly lengthy account of payments to William Parsons, including the following items :

> For making and pricking of certayne songs in English, 20s.
> For iiij psalter books, bought at Bristol, paid for every psalter book ijs. ijd.—8s. 8d.
> For two Bibles in English, and 4d. for carriage of them from Bristol, 22s. 4d.

Parsons remained at Wells until 1561, but after that date we have no record of him till his collaboration in the publication of Day's *Whole Psalms in foure partes*, in 1563, of which a second edition was published in 1565.

It may be of interest to note that this remarkable harmonized version of the Psalms included 141 compositions. Of these, as before stated, 81 are by William Parsons, while of the remainder, 27 are by Thomas Causton, 17 by J. Hake, 11 by R. Brimle, and 4 by N. Southerton.

As to Parsons's share in this harmonized Psalter—of which he was in reality the editor—Professor Wooldridge says :

> The style of Parsons is somewhat severe, sometimes even harsh, but always strong and solid. . . . The importance of this Psalter, at once the first and the most liberal of its kind, entitles it to a complete example of its workmanship. The

William Parsons

tune chosen is that to the 137th Psalm, an excellent specimen of the English imitations of the French melodies, and interesting also as being one of the two tunes which, appearing among the first printed in Crespin's edition of Sternhold, are in use at this day. It was evidently a favourite with Parsons, who has set it three times—twice placing it in the tenor, and once in the upper voice.

However, in a foot-note, he adds :

It must be confessed that this tune is more beautiful without the setting. Parsons has not only avoided every kind of modulation, but has even refused closes which the ear desires, and which he might have taken without having recourse to chromatic notes. It remained for later musicians to bring out the beauty of the melody.

I can find no trace of William Parsons after the year 1563, and evidently he died soon afterwards. His namesake, Robert Parsons, drowned himself on January 25, 1570.